MW00610836

In case of loss, please return to:

_____

_____

_____

_____

As a reward: $ _____

SAMSON

A LIFE WELL WASTED

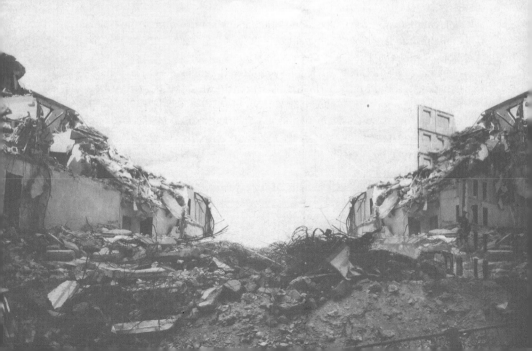

Published by LifeWay Press®
© 2013 Chip Henderson

ISBN: 978-1-4158-7239-0
Item: 005474750

Dewey Decimal Classification Number: 248.84
Subject Heading: CHRISTIAN LIFE \ SAMSON (BIBLICAL JUDGE) \ DISAPPOINTMENT

Printed in the United States of America.

Young Adult Ministry Publishing
LifeWay Church Resources
One LifeWay Plaza
Nashville, Tennessee 37234-0135

We believe that the Bible has God for its author; salvation for its end; and truth, without any mixture of error, for its matter and that all Scripture is totally true and trustworthy. To review LifeWay's doctrinal guideline, please visit *www.lifeway.com/doctrinalguideline*.

Cover design by Leigh Ann Dans and Heather Wetherington.

TABLE OF CONTENTS

ICON LEGEND

 Things to listen to

 Things to watch

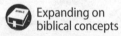 Expanding on biblical concepts

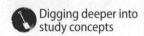 Fun facts and useful tidbits of information

Digging deeper into study concepts

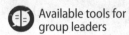 Available tools for group leaders

 On the Web

MEET THE AUTHOR
CHIP HENDERSON

My name is Chip Henderson. I grew up in Mississippi and Louisiana as the son of a pastor. I earned a degree in Communications Management from Mississippi State University. I also hold a Ph.D. in Greek and New Testament studies from New Orleans Baptist Theological Seminary. My wife, Christy, and I have been married for 21 years and have been blessed with three incredible children: Rachel, McKenzie, and Regan. I'm an avid hunter, runner, and triathlete, and I serve on the Board of Directors for the Launch Church Planting Network.

After surrendering to ministry, I served in two staff positions before beginning my first pastorate nearly 21 years ago. I have served as the senior pastor at Pinelake Church in Brandon, Mississippi, since January 1999. In that time, Pinelake has grown from an average attendance of approximately 700 people to more than 9,000 on five campuses today. I have a passion for seeing Christ bring about powerful life-change in people as well as a commitment to biblical, life-application teaching. I believe this is one way God has used me to help spark dynamic spiritual growth in the life of our church and beyond, and I'm so grateful for the opportunity to serve Him.

I wrote Samson after studying Judges 13–16 in preparation for a morning devotional for a church planting meeting in Tucson, Arizona. I read the tragic story of the incredible potential and purpose of Samson's life and watched as this God-appointed leader's life imploded on the pages of Scripture. My heart was moved as I saw a connection between the fallen leader, Samson, and the men and women of our generation. Never before have we had so much privilege, promise, and potential, and yet never before have we seen so many heartbreaking stories of lives well wasted. My hope and prayer as you engage this study is that you will avoid the mistakes that so commonly mess up our lives, and that the Lord will reveal to you the positive practices of being a spiritual influencer.

OPPORTUNITY LOST

How to waste your life

An old man had died and his funeral was in progress. The country preacher talked at length of the good traits of the deceased— what an honest man he was, and what a loving husband and kind father he was. Finally, the widow leaned over and whispered to one of her children, "Go up there and take a look in the coffin and see if that's your Pa."

I don't know about you, but I've been to a few funerals where I felt like the preacher had to make a case for why the person in the casket was a Christian. The truth is we preach our funeral while we're living.

We're all going to pass away at some point. But what if you died today? Would you be proud of what the preacher would say at your funeral? Would those who get up to speak and attest to your accomplishments have to lie or embellish? Would your family want to look in the casket and make sure they have the right person?

Throughout the coming weeks, we're going to study the life of a man whose funeral was likely no celebration. Instead it was a reflection upon a life well wasted, and it all begins in the Book of Judges.

Judges sounds like a broken record. It keeps repeating the same cycle in roughly 40-year intervals: sin, captivity, crying out to God, and then deliverance. Rinse and repeat. Joshua had died, and there was no strong man of God to lead the Israelites. The people's hearts had turned away from God, and their idolatry had led to servitude. God allowed them to be defeated and enslaved to the Canaanites and Philistines.

In Judges 13, at the beginning of Samson's story, we find the Israelites in bondage to the Philistines. The people haven't cried out to God yet, but He anticipated it in His sovereignty and began working ahead of them. In His mercy, God raised up a deliverer, a miracle child named Samson.

Samson's parents, Zoah and Manoah, who weren't supposed to be able to conceive, were told that Samson was to be a Nazirite and a deliverer for Israel. A Nazirite kept three promises: 1) He would not eat grapes or drink wine; 2) he would not touch anything dead; and 3) he would never cut his hair. The purpose of these three promises was to be completely set apart from culture—to be different in order to make a difference for God.

God's Spirit came over Samson and endowed him with supernatural strength for the purpose of delivering the nation. He is a fascinating character, one who has captured the imagination of Sunday School kids for centuries. I even named my first dog Samson.

But Samson was also a man of great weakness and foolishness.

Samson was born with incredible potential and expectations. He was a superstar in the making, and everything he needed was given to him. But Samson never lived up to the hype. Samson never engaged his purpose. He didn't deal with the wounds of his past. He kept too many secrets, refused to tame his temper, never learned to seek God, and couldn't keep his pants on. So, his story doesn't end the way one might have expected. But out of the ashes of Samson's life, during the next six sessions, I'm praying that God will raise up hope, and from examining the story of a life well wasted, that you gain a renewed sense of God's purpose for your life. I pray you know how to be in the business of living that purpose out.

YOUR STORY IS NOT YET FINISHED. GOD CAN AND WILL USE YOU, NO MATTER WHO YOU ARE OR WHAT YOU'VE DONE.

The fact remains: Your story is not yet finished. God can and will use you, no matter who you are or what you've done. Even if your story is rocky and dry. Even if you've fallen flat on your face. Even if you've managed to mess up relationship after relationship. Even if you stubbornly rebelled against God this very hour. Even if you feel like you have nowhere else to go, no one to whom you can turn, and no place that will accept you with the baggage you bring.

I believe God included stories in the Bible about people like Samson to encourage us to never lose hope. Think for a moment about all the warped people God used on the other side of failure:

- Noah hit the bottle too hard and acted like a fool before passing out. And this wasn't before the ark nor on the ark. This was after God had been good to him (Genesis 9:20-25).

- Abraham lied and said his wife was his sister (Genesis 12:10-20; 20:1-18).

- Jacob was a con artist who stole his brother's birth-right (Genesis 27:1-40).

- Moses killed a man with his bare hands (Exodus 2:11-12) and then delivered the Israelites from Egyptian slavery.

- Rahab welcomed the spies and saved her family. She is one of only five women mentioned in the lineage of Jesus Christ. But before that, she was a prostitute in the red light district of Jericho (Joshua 2).

- David, called a man after God's heart, had an adulterous affair with Bathsheba. He later wrote much of the Psalms as a result of his being restored by God (2 Samuel 11).

- Peter denied Jesus three times (Matthew 26:33-35). Later he became the Christ-appointed leader of the church.

NOBODY WANTS "AVERAGE" OR "NORMAL" OR "ORDINARY" OR "FORGETTABLE" TO BE THE DEFINING CHARACTERISTICS OF THEIR LIVES.

The Bible is full of people who messed up, yet God still used them for His glory. I don't know today where you're at spiritually, and in what part of life you're wrestling. Maybe you've messed up, and you're trying to get back on your feet. Maybe you're still on your back. Maybe you're fighting against a "normal" life, and your fear is that your funeral could be summed up with, "She was average." Nobody wants "average" or "normal" or "ordinary" or "forgettable" to be the defining characteristics of their lives. In fact, you don't have to do bad things to waste your life. Sometimes life is wasted on just being "normal."

Whether you feel like you've already wasted countless seasons, you feel like you're right in the middle of those wasted seasons, or you're seeking after a story that's extraordinary, God has something to say to you through the life of Samson.

Through his life, we'll see a life well wasted.

My prayer is that you'd not waste yours.

PAST
REVISITED

Don't deal with your
daddy issues.

Samson was a God-appointed leader of the Israelites, set apart to protect and defend them from outside insurgents. Yet because he refused to adhere to the purposes God had laid before him, Samson ultimately wasted his life. In this session we'll take a look at the events leading up to Samson's birth and the family of origin issues that would later affect his decisions—decisions that eventually led to his demise. Samson's story serves as a word of caution for us all. We are ultimately responsible for whether or not our lives glorify God.

UNDERSTANDING ISRAEL'S PAST

In order to understand where we're going, we have to first grasp where we've been. Before we examine Samson's life, let's consider the context of the culture in which he was born. The Book of Judges picks up Israel's story where the Book of Joshua ends, almost 300 years prior to Samson's birth. Under Joshua, Moses' apprentice, the Israelites were obedient and faithful to God.

> "Joshua sent the people away, and the Israelites went to take possession of the land, each to his own inheritance. The people worshiped the LORD throughout Joshua's lifetime and during the lifetimes of the elders who outlived Joshua. They had seen all the LORD's great works He had done for Israel. Joshua son of Nun, the servant of the LORD, died at the age of 110" (Judges 2:6-8).

What stands out to you about Joshua's leadership from these verses?

After Joshua's death, the judges took over as Israel's divinely-appointed leadership. The period of judges extended from the death of Joshua (when Israel inhabited the promised land) until the era of Eli and Samuel (the beginning of monarchy). Two key factors controlled Israel's history during this period.

1. The generation after Joshua's death didn't know God at all.
The first factor was Israel's ongoing tendency to break the most important commandment in the Bible, as the people replaced their love for and worship of the Lord with the worship of their pagan neighbors' false gods. (After the incident with the golden calf, Moses warned the people to guard themselves against any covenants with the Canaanite people [Exodus 34:15-16]. They did not heed the warning.) This sin resulted in God punishing His people, most often through the use of invading armies:

 Watch the *Samson* video for Session 1, available at *threadsmedia.com/samson*.

 Samson is best known for his superhuman strength and his betrayal by Delilah.

"That whole generation was also gathered to their ancestors. After them another generation rose up who did not know the LORD or the works He had done for Israel. The Israelites did what was evil in the LORD's sight. They worshiped the Baals and abandoned the LORD, the God of their fathers, who had brought them out of Egypt. They went after other gods from the surrounding peoples and bowed down to them. They infuriated the LORD, for they abandoned Him and worshiped Baal and the Ashtoreths. The LORD's anger burned against Israel, and He handed them over to marauders who raided them. He sold them to the enemies around them, and they could no longer resist their enemies. Whenever the Israelites went out, the LORD was against them and brought disaster on them, just as He had promised and sworn to them. So they suffered greatly" (Judges 2:10-15).

When have you seen sin lead to a downward spiral in the life of a person, family, or community?

The Israelites chasing after other gods has been called spiritual adultery. Describe a time when you were unfaithful to God. How did you restore the relationship?

2. The Israelites weren't protected from invasions.

Israel was one nation without a central government. They did not have a king, president, or other form of central leadership. Instead, the nation's key societal structures were tribes, clans, and families. The lack of central government meant the nation's citizens paid no taxes, yet it also meant they had no national army to respond to attacks or invasions from other groups or nations. Israel lacked a professional fighting force *and* a leader responsible for defending the nation. Thus, after God had sufficiently chastened His people (like in v. 15 above), He would raise up a temporary regional leader to carry out His judgments against the invaders:

> "The LORD raised up judges, who saved them from the power of their marauders" (v. 16).

These divinely-appointed agents were the 12 judges, or governors, in the Book of Judges: Othniel, Ehud, Shamgar, Deborah and Barak (two people counted as one judgeship), Gideon, Tola, Jair, Jephthah, Ibzan, Elon, Abdon, and our person of interest, Samson. All the judges were instruments in the hands of God; He used them to deliver His people. They enforced the covenant (2:19), provided military leadership (3:10), and made judicial decisions (4:5). In short, the judges were military and civic leaders.[1]

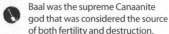 Baal was the supreme Canaanite god that was considered the source of both fertility and destruction.

With the death of Abdon, the second-to-last judge, the Israelites had further deviated from God's plan. For the seventh and final time in Judges, the writer recorded these words:

> **"The Israelites again did what was evil in the LORD's sight, so the LORD handed them over to the Philistines 40 years" (Judges 13:1).**

The text doesn't mention that the Israelites cried out to God for deliverance while in the hands of the Philistines, yet He still appointed a new judge, a deliverer, chosen to once again spiritually refocus and physically protect Israel. Enter Samson, the first Israelite to lead God's people against the Philistines.

THE BIRTH OF SAMSON

Samson was a gift of God to an otherwise childless couple.

> **"There was a certain man from Zorah, from the family of Dan, whose name was Manoah; his wife was unable to conceive and had no children. The Angel of the LORD appeared to the woman and said to her, 'It is true that you are unable to conceive and have no children, but you will conceive and give birth to a son. Now please be careful not to drink wine or beer, or to eat anything unclean; for indeed, you will conceive and give birth to a son. You must never cut his hair, because the boy will be a Nazirite to God from birth, and he will begin to save Israel from the power of the Philistines.' Then the woman went and told her husband, 'A man of God came to me. He looked like the awe-inspiring Angel of God. I didn't ask Him where He came from, and He didn't tell me His name. He said to me, "You will conceive and give birth to a son. Therefore, do not drink wine or beer, and do not eat anything unclean, because the boy will be a Nazirite to God from birth until the day of his death"'" (Judges 13:2-7).**

How did the Lord show He was planning to use Samson to accomplish His purposes?

Born during spiritual chaos and impending warfare, Samson's parents followed the angel's instructions and raised him as a Nazirite, a person under a vow to serve God in a special way—either for a limited purpose or for a lifelong commitment. In Samson's case, he was under a lifelong vow from birth.

Nazirites were to abstain from three actions: 1) consuming wine and other grape-related products, 2) cutting their hair, and 3) touching the deceased. (Numbers 6:1-21

 The Book of Judges is the second of four books known as the Former Prophets: Joshua, Judges, Samuel, and Kings.

 The circumstances surrounding Samson's birth are reminiscent of Sarah in Genesis 11:30, raising expectations of the birth of a child having great significance to God's plan.

further explains the intricacies of this vow.) These three restrictions—diet, appearance, and associations—served as a means for Samson to remain devoted to God. As we'll later find, despite Samson's Nazirite status, he struggled with a self-centered focus. It seems Samson's spiritual devotion was reduced to religious legalism: a list of "don'ts." He completely missed the whole point of the vow he was to keep: to be separated for a godly task, loving, and honoring Him above all. Let's explore some reasons for Samson's inability and/or unwillingness to follow God's instructions.

THE MANOAH AFFECT

First things first, I believe Samson's father, Manoah, was a spiritual man. Judges 13–14 reveals that Samson's dad was a decent, godly man with good intentions. In a day and time when no one honored the Lord and every man did what was right in his own eyes, here was a man and his wife who prayed and did their best to obey. But Manoah was not perfect. The Book of Judges reveals deficiencies in Manoah that negatively affected Samson. True, Manoah was not a bad man. God Himself trusted Manoah to raise up Samson. But Manoah made several key mistakes that I believe wounded his impressionable son.

Manoah failed to see God.

In simple terms, Manoah lacked faith. Samson was born into a long line of Israelites who failed to be obedient and faithful to God. This cycle of sin had a huge impact on the relationship between Manoah and his son Samson. Here we find a family trying to follow God in a messed up world. And obviously they aren't perfect.

> "Manoah prayed to the LORD and said, 'Please Lord, let the man of God you sent come again to us and teach us what we should do for the boy who will be born.' God listened to Manoah, and the Angel of God came again to the woman. She was sitting in the field, and her husband Manoah was not with her. The woman ran quickly to her husband and told him, 'The man who came to me today has just come back!' So Manoah got up and followed his wife. When he came to the man, he asked, 'Are You the man who spoke to my wife?' 'I am,' He said. Then Manoah asked, 'When Your words come true, what will the boy's responsibilities and mission be?' The Angel of the LORD answered Manoah, 'Your wife needs to do everything I told her. She must not eat anything that comes from the grapevine or drink wine or beer. And she must not eat anything unclean. Your wife must do everything I have commanded her'" (Judges 13:8-14).

Here we find Manoah praying to God, which is clearly a good thing, and God answered. But even this second time, the angel didn't appear to Manoah, but to his wife. Perhaps Manoah couldn't believe what his wife had told him, so he asked for a repeat performance for confirmation. Or possibly he was jealous that the angel first appeared to his wife rather

---

 John the Baptist (Luke 1:15-17) is another prominent example of someone under a lifelong Nazirite vow.

 In order for the Israelites to satisfy the demands of the Lord, it was essential for every Israelite family to choose obedience to Him (Joshua 24:15).

than to him. It's significant to note that, at this point, nothing was required of Manoah, just of his wife. Manoah's responsibility and accountability would come later.

> "'Please stay here,' Manoah told Him, 'and we will prepare a young goat for You.' The Angel of the LORD said to him, 'If I stay, I won't eat your food. But if you want to prepare a burnt offering, offer it to the LORD.' For Manoah did not know He was the Angel of the LORD. Then Manoah said to Him, 'What is Your name, so that we may honor You when Your words come true?' 'Why do you ask My name,' the Angel of the LORD asked him, 'since it is wonderful.' Manoah took a young goat and a grain offering and offered them on a rock to the LORD, and He did a wonderful thing while Manoah and his wife were watching. When the flame went up from the altar to the sky, the Angel of the LORD went up in its flame. When Manoah and his wife saw this, they fell facedown on the ground. The Angel of the LORD did not appear again to Manoah and his wife. Then Manoah realized that it was the Angel of the LORD. 'We're going to die,' he said to his wife, 'because we have seen God!' But his wife said to him, 'If the LORD had intended to kill us, He wouldn't have accepted the burnt offering and the grain offering from us, and He would not have shown us all these things or spoken to us now like this.' So the woman gave birth to a son and named him Samson. The boy grew, and the LORD blessed him. Then the Spirit of the LORD began to direct him in the Camp of Dan, between Zorah and Eshtaol" (Judges 13:15-25).

Manoah offered the Angel of the LORD a meal, but the messenger told him to offer the lamb to God as a sacrifice. When Manoah made the sacrifice, the messenger worked wonders and then spectacularly ascended to heaven in a flame. Samson's parents finally realized this was an Angel of the LORD, and Manoah's first response was fear. It took his wife's prompting for Manoah to understand that God wouldn't kill the father of the person He was raising up to lead the Israelites.

God showed up, but Manoah missed it.

What did Manoah do that left him unprepared to hear from God?

— What circumstances in your life distract you from God? What are some things you do (or don't do) that focus you for worship?

....

 Samson's name, translated from Hebrew, means "bright as the sun" or "sun child."

How can you prepare yourself to hear from God minute-by-minute, hour-by-hour?

Manoah lacked spiritual leadership.

Just as Samson's father had faults, so likely did Manoah's. The lack of spiritual leadership was a big issue for the Israelites during the time of the judges. They lacked a positive central authority figure to show them the way they should go. And that's just like many of us. Sometimes we lack the godly guidance of a parental role model. A man who wasn't led well has a difficult time leading others well because he hasn't seen the example.

Samson was an only child born late in his parent's lives—a perfect recipe for the raising of a spoiled child. God's Spirit had begun stirring within Samson to prepare for battle with the Philistines, but instead of killing them, he fell in love with one.

> **"Samson went down to Timnah and saw a young Philistine woman there. He went back and told his father and his mother: 'I have seen a young Philistine woman in Timnah. Now get her for me as a wife'"** (Judges 14:1-2).

Samson shouldn't have been going down to see the Philistines in the first place. The Philistines were enemies of both Israel and God. Samson had no self-control, presumably because he lacked parental discipline and authority. Scripture says Samson "told his father and mother." In other words, he chose to stand boldly opposed to his parents (and God) as he announced his intentions. He then commanded his parents to "get her," or "buy her" (a likely reference to her dowry).

- Has there ever been a time in your life when you've wanted something that wasn't good for you? Did God allow you to have that? Why or why not?

- Knowing what you know now, what would you tell the "younger you" before that decision?

For us guys, we typically aren't humble enough to admit when we don't know the right choice to make (Come on, we won't even stop and ask for directions!), and Samson was prototypical. But here, we get the sense that Samson is a spoiled only child, telling his parents what to do.

 In 2012, a Samson mosaic was discovered during the excavation of a Byzantine-era synagogue in Galilee.

"But his father and mother said to him, 'Can't you find a young woman among your relatives or among any of our people? Must you go to the uncircumcised Philistines for a wife?' But Samson told his father, 'Get her for me, because I want her' Now his father and mother did not know this was from the LORD, who was seeking an occasion against the Philistines. At that time, the Philistines were ruling over Israel" (Judges 14:3-4).

Samson's parents objected to his demands: "You can't find a girlfriend among our people?" To be honest with you, that response bothers me. Parenting involves establishing clear boundaries for our children when they step out of line. Samson was clearly being ruled by what he saw—a fatal flaw that became a major character defect throughout his life—in part because his parents failed to confront him. Manoah should have said, "Samson, men of God are not ruled by their eyes, appetites, and desires, but by God's Word and God's purpose." Just as God punishes those He loves, so are parents to reprimand and guide their children:

"My son, do not take the Lord's discipline lightly or faint when you are reproved by Him, for the Lord disciplines the one He loves and punishes every son He receives" (Hebrews 12:5-6).

How can discipline actually be a form of mercy?

How could God's "no" actually be an example of His love for us? Can you think of times in your life where God said no to you? How did it turn out?

I don't know about you, but my parents wouldn't let me go certain places—dances, night-clubs, parties, that kind of stuff. Some may call it sheltered, but the truth is they were shielding me from the way they didn't want me to live my life.

What were some things you weren't allowed to do? places you couldn't go?

Do you ever wish your parents had told you no more often? How would that have saved you mistakes and heartaches?

Samson didn't know how to act when things didn't go his way. (This is a theme we'll see several more times throughout his life.) Forgetting His God-given gifts and responsibilities, Samson thought everything revolved around him. He saw his strength as a way to get what he wanted: women. Samson had no respect for authority in his life. He rejected his parents' opinions, and he brought them shame with his marriage to a Philistine woman. But more importantly, he didn't respect God's authority either. God's plan was clear, but Samson didn't seem to care.

One of the reasons we give a child rules and consequences is so that they know and respect God's rules and consequences. We may think we're doing our kids a favor by giving them everything they want, but it's not true. What they need—and what we needed—is godly leadership and guidance.

Samson, as we'll discover, never got past his past. He ended up wasting his life and wounding others in the process. Maybe you recognize that some of the negative behavior in your life, the problems you're facing right now, stem from deep-seated roots. Our parents shape our hearts, our minds, our character, and our lives.

There's no doubt that your father, mother, grandparent, or another person in your life growing up significantly marked you and shaped who you've become. Discovering the ways you've been shaped, both positively and negatively, may be the most important part of this study for you.

What was your relationship with your parents like? What are some qualities about your father and mother you admired? Avoided?

Besides your parents or grandparents, who else significantly invested in your life?

WHAT WE CAN LEARN FROM MANOAH

So, why pick on Manoah? Surely Samson's mother got plenty of things wrong. Likely she did, but my answer is simple: A father's spiritual depth and emotional involvement has a profound impact on his children. Scripture directly addresses fathers for the responsibility of rearing children. They are held accountable for this responsibility because a father's actions today directly impact his children's tomorrow. Manoah was responsible for giving Samson spiritual guidance. Yet how could Manoah truly have provided vision for his son if he didn't have it himself?

 Listen to "Beauty in the Broken" by Hyland, "Not for a Moment (After All)" by Meredith Andrews, and "Losing" by Tenth Avenue North from the *Samson* playlist, available at *threadsmedia.com/samson*.

"If people can't see what God is doing, they stumble all over themselves; But when they attend to what he reveals, they are most blessed" (Proverbs 29:18, MSG).

What was/is your father's vision for your life? Was it based on biblical guidance?

For better or worse, we become like our fathers. Sometimes it's for better: Our dads pass on positive virtues like honesty, integrity, a sense of humor, a good work ethic, a spiritual foundation, or devotion to family. But at other times it's for worse: Our father's flaws and weaknesses adversely impact us and they pass on some bad actions, attitudes, dispositions, or even character flaws. Sometimes these are called "daddy wounds." A counselor might call them "family of origin issues." These wounds usually describe some minor or major deficiencies in us that need to be addressed and healed. We often hear this brushed aside as, "I do [insert flaw here] because of the way I was raised," without taking personal responsibility of the issue at hand. Consider what research has shown about the positive developmental depth to which a father's presence and involvement affects his children.

- According to T. Berry Brazelton, pediatrician, author, and former clinical professor of Pediatrics Emeritus at Harvard Medical School, "a father's involvement with a child increases the child's IQ, the child's motivation to learn, and the child's self-confidence. In addition, children with involved dads are more likely to develop a sense of humor as well as an 'inner excitement.'"[2]

- At the 2008 First National Research Conference in Massachusetts, a soon-to-be postdoctoral research associate at Princeton University explained, "Children were indeed 'better off' the longer the biological father lived in the household. They found that an additional 5 years living with a biological father reduced the probability of outcomes such as smoking, drinking, convictions, marijuana use and pre-marital sexual activity."[3]

- Adolescents who strongly identified with their fathers were 80 percent less likely to have been in jail and 75 percent less likely to become unwed parents.[4]

Overall, when a father is present, active, and attached to his children, it's easy to see the positive influence on the lives of his family. However, just as in Manoah's case, fathers aren't perfect. Mistakes are made, and damage is done. Richard Innes, in the article "Healing a Man's Father Wound" says,

"Ask a hundred men how many felt close to and affirmed by their fathers and you will see about three or four hands raised. Herein lays the secret of so much

 Effective fathers lead by demonstrating their devotion, discipline, and worship to their families.[5]

of our relational and emotional distress. The father-wound that injured our masculine soul is because we never felt close to or loved by our father. And that wound desperately needs to be healed. (The same principle also applies to women who carry a deep father-wound.)"[6]

Author Mike Genung, in an article called "Healing Father Wounds," describes three ways our fathers wound us.[7] We can be wounded by . . .

1. Withdrawn, passive fathers

These are men who were physically present but "missing in action" emotionally. A father's silence can be just as devastating as any kind of abuse; it leaves a child subconsciously or consciously wondering, *Doesn't he care? Does he really love me? Am I worthy of being loved?*

Yes, a physical presence is essential to families. However, much more than taking residence is required. Fathers are biblically mandated to provide financial and emotional support, physical assistance and security, and leadership for their wives and children. They are called to be engaged in the inner workings of the family:

> **"Husbands, love your wives, just as Christ loved the church and gave Himself for her . . . husbands are to love their wives as their own bodies. He who loves his wife loves himself. For no one ever hates his own flesh but provides and cares for it" (Ephesians 5:25,28-29).**

> **"Fathers, don't stir up anger in your children, but bring them up in the training and instruction of the Lord" (Ephesians 6:4).**

How would you describe the level of your father's engagement to your family? How has that role changed as you've gotten older?

If you're a parent (or want to be in the future) what words and actions display to your children that you're engaged? What's the antithesis of engagement?

2. Absent fathers

When a father leaves young children, the children are profoundly impacted. In spite of what a father may say or the time on the weekends he may spend with his kids, the roaring silence of Dad's missing presence during the week, months, or years causes a child to think, *Surely he wouldn't have left if he loved me. Maybe if I was good enough he'd still be around.*

 "Kids spell love T-I-M-E." —Dr. Ken Canfield, founder and president, National Center for Fathering[8]

A father's absence implies that the child wasn't worth the sacrifice, and that implication becomes imbedded into the thread of that child's being.

This is a growing trend in our world. It's been estimated that 85 percent of single parents are women. Just in the United States, approximately 24 million children (34 percent) live absent their biological fathers.[9] Never before have we seen so many fathers not a part of their childrens' lives. This lack of involvement in a God-ordained role is reshaping and redefining the American family. According to the *Fragile Families Journal:*

> "As rates of nonmarital childbirth have increased in the United States in the past half-century, a new family type, the fragile family, has emerged. Fragile families, which are formed as the result of a nonmarital birth, include cohabiting couples as well as noncohabiting, single mothers. Such families evoke public concern in part because they are more impoverished and endure more material hardship than married-parent families and have fewer sources of economic support."[10]

What short- and long-term effects do you see from so many children growing up without their fathers?

Children of absent fathers have a lot to overcome.

- They're two to three times more likely to be poor, abuse drugs and alcohol, experience physical, emotional, or educational neglect, and engage in criminal activity.[11]
- Young fathers were also less likely to be living with their children if their own fathers had not lived in residence with them throughout childhood.[12]
- Women whose parents separated between birth and 6 years old experienced more than four times the risk of early sexual intercourse, and two and a half times higher risk of early pregnancy when compared to women in intact families.[13]
- 63 percent of youth suicides are from fatherless homes.[14]
- 90 percent of homeless and runaway children are without fathers.[15]
- 71 percent of high school dropouts come from fatherless homes.[16]

If your father was absent while growing up, how has that shaped your life?

 If your earthly father doesn't measure up, trust in Him who heals wounds and will never let us down (Psalm 103:13; Romans 8:15; Hebrews 13:5).

What negative effects have you been able to identify from his absence?

If your father was present and engaged, what positive aspects of your life today can be attributed to your relationship with him?

3. Abusive fathers

For those who've been physically, psychologically, or even sexually abused by a parent, having a passive father would likely have been a blessing. The message of worthlessness has violently shaped them into a distorted truth of their childhood innocence. When the man or woman who should've communicated beauty, honor, respect, and strength twists that truth, the results can be disastrous. Receiving love and affection is almost impossible as hopelessness, despair, and rage set in. It's difficult—if not impossible—to receive love from someone else when the most important person in our lives indicated our severe lack of worth.

While abuse often goes unreported, here's what we do know:

- 1 in 10 kids in the United States were abused in 2010. In the same year, 1,560 children died from their injuries or neglect.

- Almost 80 percent (79.4 percent) of all child fatalities due to abuse were younger than 4 years old.

- 32.6 percent of child fatalities are attributed to neglect.

- 84.2 percent of perpetrators were the biological parent of the abused and/or neglected child.

- The average response time by authorities after suspected abuse is reported is 61 hours or 2.5 days.

- Victimization was split between the sexes, with boys accounting for 48.5 percent and girls accounting for 51.2 percent.[17]

Did you experience any of the above, whether directly or indirectly? At what age(s)? How has that marked you?

 Leading a group? Find extra questions and teaching tools in the leader kit, available for purchase at *threadsmedia.com/samson*.

Kids wounded in any of these ways often seek attention, because in their minds any attention—even bad attention—is better than nothing. For example, little girls give themselves to boys at an early age, and some for the rest of their lives because they want to feel beautiful, wanted, and loved. Boys often exert their pent-up aggression by starting fights, looking to prove their manhood by beating somebody up.

As adults, some cover their wounds with work. The drive to be successful makes them feel like they matter. Some become codependent, while others can't stand the thought of being alone. Others turn to sports, sex—whether "real" or "virtual"—food, alcohol, or drugs, all trying to fill the void and numb the pain.

If you have deep wounds from your past, what have you used as an escape and/or to get attention?

Take a moment to pray, asking God to reveal to you ways in which you may have been wounded by your father, mother, or guardian. Ask God to heal you from your past and empower you to stop the cycle of hurt.

HOW DO YOU GET OVER A DADDY WOUND?
If you've found that you carry wounds from your past that need healing, here are some ways that you can begin to move forward.

1. Own that you have issues.
Investigate and see what negative qualities, habits, or hang-ups you got from your parents. See where your wound may show itself: alcohol and/or drug abuse, anger issues, passive aggressive behavior when things don't go your way, an inability to admit you are wrong, wallowing in past failures, a tendency toward pride, passivity, or control, and so forth.

> **"If we say, 'We have no sin,' we are deceiving ourselves, and the truth is not in us" (1 John 1:8).**

2. Take responsibility for your own actions.
Each of us is responsible for our own sins and behavior. We may be wounded by a problem past, but our present decisions aren't the fault of our fathers. We need to stop blaming our present problems on our past pain.

....

 One of the best ways to heal from your own wounds is to help others. If you're not a parent, sign up to be a Big Brother or Big Sister at *bbbs.org*. The next generation needs caring, committed people to stand in the gap.

Instead of casting blame, maybe, just maybe, God could be up to something bigger. Even when people have sinned against us, God can shape us and use the most horrific sins to write a beautiful story.

> "Praise the God and Father of our Lord Jesus Christ, the Father of mercies and the God of all comfort. He comforts us in all our affliction, so that we may be able to comfort those who are in any kind of affliction, through the comfort we ourselves receive from God. For as the sufferings of Christ overflow to us, so through Christ our comfort also overflows. If we are afflicted, it is for your comfort and salvation. If we are comforted, it is for your comfort, which is experienced in your endurance of the same sufferings that we suffer. And our hope for you is firm, because we know that as you share in the sufferings, so you will share in the comfort" (2 Corinthians 1:3-7).

> "Fathers are not to be put to death for their children or children for their fathers; each person will be put to death for his own sin" (Deuteronomy 24:16).

3. Claim the forgiveness and power of God to change you in Christ.

If God has forgiven you, you're a new creation with renewed hope and a boatload of grace and mercy—more than you could ever exhaust. And with the same power that raised Christ from the dead, you're given the freedom to live a new life:

> "You took off your former way of life, the old self that is corrupted by deceitful desires; you are being renewed in the spirit of your minds; you put on the new self, the one created according to God's likeness in righteousness and purity of the truth" (Ephesians 4:22-24).

> "Therefore, if anyone is in Christ, he is a new creation; old things have passed away, and look, new things have come" (2 Corinthians 5:17).

4. Find your value and meaning in Christ.

The question of whether or not you matter has already been answered. The place where you find love, rest, and peace is in Jesus. Replace the lies perpetrated by your earthly father with the truth of your Heavenly Father. God gave His Son so that you could be adopted into His family. He loves you that much.

> "Look at how great a love the Father has given us that we should be called God's children. And we are!" (1 John 3:1a).

 John 14:1-4 explains that by believing in Christ we are empowered to become children of God, members of His household, and have relationship with the Father.

5. Forgive the person who wronged you.
When we hold onto bitterness, resentment, and hatred, we allow our pasts to dictate our future, and we offer the enemy a perfect platform to exercise dominion in our lives.

There are no perfect fathers. So let your dad go. Even if your father is deceased, write him a letter explaining your hurt. Forgive him in Jesus' name. Say, "I bless you, pray for you, and want to have a healthy relationship with you if at all possible." Then regardless of his response, let it go.

> **"And be kind and compassionate to one another, forgiving one another, just as God also forgave you in Christ" (Ephesians 4:32).**

Which of the above verses most resonates with where you find yourself right now?

What is most difficult about forgiving someone who has hurt you deeply?

The sad and twisted part of parental wounds is not only that our lives are affected, but that we often repeat the pattern as we transition to parenthood.

STOP THE CYCLE OF DYSFUNCTION
One of the saddest verses in the Bible is found just prior to the story of Samson:

> **"That whole generation was also gathered to their ancestors. After them another generation rose up who did not know the LORD or the works He had done for Israel" (Judges 2:10).**

It's possible for a generation to completely lose sight of God—His power, His grace, His love, and His forgiveness. But it's also possible for that trend to be reversed. And it starts with you! If you're currently a parent or ever plan to be, let's discuss some ways you can become an effective spiritual leader in your own household:

1. Let your family see you read the Bible. Let them hear you pray. Let them see you live with integrity and consistency. Let them go with you when you minister to someone in need. Let them catch you doing the right thing, especially in difficult or frustrating situations.

2. Consistently discipline in your home (Ephesians 6:4). Here's a truth you know: Doing bad things in life brings pain. That doesn't mean you beat your kids. In fact, it's quite

---

 Resources for further study: *Wild at Heart* by John Eldredge, *Breaking Free* by Beth Moore, and *The Parent Adventure* by Rodney and Selma Wilson

the opposite. You spare the rod and spoil the child for sure. But that's only one side of discipline. The real power is not in bringing pain when they do bad but in bringing blessing when they do good. Love your kids. Brag on their good behavior. Laugh with them. Catch them doing the right things, and praise them for it.

3. Tell your kids you're sorry. When you mess up, don't cover it up. Be honest, and ask for forgiveness. Show them how to act when they do things they're not proud of.

4. Bless your child. Gary Smalley and John Trent in their book, *The Blessing,* say that there are five things children need from their dads: "meaningful touch" (to be hugged and touched in a non-sexual and non-violent way); "spoken words" (to tell them you love them and are proud of them); "expressing high value" (telling them they matter, they're special, and they have great qualities); "picturing a special future" (ensuring they know that they are filled with potential, possessing unique gifts and capabilities that God is going to use one day to bless others); and "an active commitment" (repeating these four things consistently and often).[18]

Parents: What can you do now to begin making these traits a reality in your home?

Non-parents: What step(s) can you take right now to a) be ready if God blesses you with children? b) help other parents in their God-given role? How can you personally help care for the next generation of kids?

APPLY TO LIFE

> **CONNECT:** Approach someone you know and trust well. Buy that person a cup of coffee and ask if you can share and talk through some wounds you've received from your parents. If you haven't yet identified these wounds, ask your friend to help you see what you can't see.

> **STUDY:** Begin this week to study Samson's failures. In this lesson, we explored Samson's family of origin that led him down a dangerous path. Write down (below) the times when Samson messed up. Do you see a pattern? What was the root of Samson's sin?

> **LISTEN:** Purchase "Beauty in the Broken" by Hyland, "Not for a Moment (After All)" by Meredith Andrews, and "Losing" by Tenth Avenue North (see the playlist at *threadsmedia. com/samson*). Add these to your regular mix of music throughout the week so that you'll be reminded to continue thinking about God's ability to heal our pasts.

LIES
UNTOLD

Don't tell the truth.

The headline read, "Study: 100 percent of Americans lead secret lives." The story from *The Onion*, an online news source, cited a study released by the University of California-Berkeley that "100 percent of Americans fail to disclose the full truth about what they think and do in private."

The article continues, "'While startling and often embarrassing revelations about the private lives of politicians, professional athletes, and celebrities surface on a routine basis, our research indicates that Americans out of the public eye also have a lot to hide,' said Berkeley sociology professor Dr. Mia L. Greene, who headed the 10-year study. 'Surprisingly, famous people aren't the only ones participating in shady business dealings, substance abuse, and peculiar sexual activities.'" Even the average person engages "in strange and obsessive behavior that, if revealed, would humiliate them."[1]

Though *The Onion* isn't a legitimate news source, it does poke fun at an uncomfortable truth. Everyone has secrets; everyone tries to hide the parts of themselves that shame them. Is that really true? Does *everybody* have secrets?

How do you respond to this article? Are there parts of your personal life that you wouldn't want leaked to the tabloids?

What you do in private matters because it reveals the true you. My prayer for you while working through this session is that you will learn from Samson's secrecy and the effect his private sins had on his life. Together we can commit to reversing his curse and live lives that publicly and privately honor God.

SAMSON'S SECRET LIFE

Samson definitely had his fair share of secrets. He was a man of incredible physical strength, but he tried to hide his personal and spiritual weaknesses. Samson failed to follow the demands of his Nazirite vow and generally made poor choices when pressed by his enemies or led on by lust. But it was his uncontrolled spirit—how he acted in those moments when no one was around—that paved the way for his public failure.

> **"Samson went down to Timnah with his father and mother and came to the vineyards of Timnah. Suddenly a young lion came roaring at him, the Spirit of the LORD took control of him, and he tore the lion apart with his bare hands as he might have torn a young goat. But he did not tell his father or mother what he had done. Then he went and spoke to the woman, because Samson wanted her" (Judges 14:5-7).**

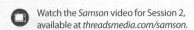 Watch the *Samson* video for Session 2, available at *threadsmedia.com/samson*.

You can bet that if something this extraordinary happened to me, I would tell everyone I know. But Samson had a superhuman encounter with a lion, and he didn't tell anyone about it. He seems to have withheld the information intentionally. For whatever reason, he didn't want anyone to know he had been in the vineyard. Going to the vineyard doesn't automatically mean Samson was guilty of breaking his Nazirite vow not to drink wine, but this story doesn't read like he's innocent either.

In the last session, we read that Samson demanded his parents go get the girl he desired. He wanted them to know he was in love with a Philistine "fox," but didn't want them to know he ravaged a roaring lion. Samson may not have told a direct lie, but he was guilty of the sin of omission.

Can you remember ever withholding information from your parents to avoid the consequences of your actions? How did it turn out?

If the first encounter with a lion was an "accident," the second encounter was Samson's fault, without a doubt:

> **"After some time, when he returned to get her, he left the road to see the lion's carcass, and there was a swarm of bees with honey in the carcass"** (Judges 14:8).

Samson wanted to see what had happened to the animal he destroyed with his bare hands. Like all of us at times, curiosity and pride got the best of him. Had he just looked, pride would have been all he was guilty of, but Samson didn't stop there.

Samson's olfactory system kicked in—his sense of smell. Something inside his brain caused his saliva glands to secrete, and his mouth started watering. His stomach began growling, and he felt hungry. Samson's body began working against his brain, all because of an "innocent" glance. He knew what he shouldn't do, but in the moment of temptation, his mind was racing against him.

The longer you look at what's forbidden, the closer you come to craving it and eventually caving to it. That's the way it is with any temptation. The longer you linger, the lower you go.

In what areas of your life are you tempted to "just look" at something or someone? What words or phrases do you use, or have you heard others use, to justify "just looking"?

 Lions, a proverbial symbol for strength, are mentioned approximately 135 times in the Old Testament.

Samson went to the see the lion's carcass, but was overcome with temptation. He wasn't prepared for the carcass to have a swarm of bees in it. In that moment, Samson had to choose between walking away or breaking his vow:

> "He must not go near a dead body during the time he consecrates himself to the LORD. He is not to defile himself for his father or mother, or his brother or sister, when they die, because the hair consecrated to his God is on his head. He is holy to the LORD during the time of consecration" (Numbers 6:6-8).

Giving in to the temptation, Samson bent down and cupped his hands to eat a fist full of forbidden honey.

> "He scooped some honey into his hands and ate it as he went along. . . . " (Judges 14:9a).

Samson's decision had further ramifications than breaking his Nazirite vow.

> " . . . When he returned to his father and mother, he gave some to them and they ate it. But he did not tell them that he had scooped the honey from the lion's carcass" (Judges 14:9b).

Again we see that Samson was guilty of the sin of omission, withholding critical information from his parents and compromising their religious cleanliness. Even if they never asked him where the honey came from—meaning he didn't have to directly lie—he still defiled them by serving them honey from a corpse. We'll read later that Samson never told his parents the truth, whether they asked or not, and this second sin of omission would catch up with him.

> "Since you put away lying, Speak the truth, each one to his neighbor, because we are members of one another" (Ephesians 4:25).

Paul urged us to put off our old, sin nature, and to put on our new selves in holiness. This verse is often referred to as Paul's "put off/put on" principle.

How does this principle apply to lies of omission like Samson committed?

Are there circumstances when lies of omission or "white" lies are appropriate? Explain your response.

If telling the truth is a fruit of a regenerated person, to whom do you need to tell the truth today? Write his or her name below.

How many times have you said a little white lie? *I was an all-star on my high school football team. I'd love to go volunteer with you, but I've had plans for weeks. No officer, I didn't realize I was going over the speed limit. It's not you, it's me. Of course you look awesome in that dress! I sent you an e-mail invite; you didn't get it? I would've been on time but there was a wreck on the interstate. This gift is exactly what I wanted. You're such a good cook. I only bought it because it was on sale. Of course I wanted a purple basket-weaving set; I love it!* And often we've convinced ourselves that little white lies are OK. They ease us out of awkward conversations or maintain the feelings of another person.

But maybe your truth is more complicated.

Maybe you've been keeping secrets from someone you love. Maybe you've been lying to make yourself feel better. Or maybe you've just plain been lying to yourself. We've all caught ourselves in little white lies, told stories that make us look better, said things that weren't true, or made mistakes we don't want shared with the world. So let's stop kidding ourselves. What we say and do matters.

HIDDEN AGENDAS

We often do the same thing as Samson, allowing curiosity and arrogance to get the best of us. We carry on conversations with a coworker that are full of innuendo and flirtation. *I'm not hurting anyone,* we think. *I'm just messing around. Sure, we text sometimes, but it's innocent, I swear!* We peek at pictures on the Internet. *It's no big deal. It's not like it's lusting, right? Just a quick look.* Or we convince ourselves that temptation is OK, regardless of what our credit card bills look like: *The store is having a great sale. Besides, just one more pair won't matter. I'm just gonna go look.*

Temptation itself is not a sin, but giving in to the temptation is. Hebrews 4 reminds us that Jesus was tempted to sin but didn't give in.

 Struggling with looking at inappropriate things on the Internet? Get some help! Here are a few software recommendations: XXX Church (*x3watch.com*), Covenant Eyes (*covenanteyes.com*), or Safe Eyes (*internetsafety.com/safeeyes*).

"For we do not have a high priest who is unable to sympathize with our weaknesses, but One who has been tested in every way as we are, yet without sin. Therefore let us approach the throne of grace with boldness, so that we may receive mercy and find grace to help us at the proper time" (vv. 15-16).

The choice is ours whether we give in to temptations or not.

Where's the line between temptation and sin? How do you know when you've crossed that line?

We typically think of lust as a sexual desire for another person. What else do people lust for?

A lot of people are hiding things in their lives. Are you erasing the history on your computer, padding your expense report, lying to someone about where you're going and what you're doing? Are you deleting calls and texts and making sure you beat your spouse to the mailbox for the cell phone bill? Are you convincing yourself that "what happens in Vegas"—or Birmingham, Atlanta, Chicago, New York, Dallas, Memphis, Panama City Beach, Rome, Paris, or Stockholm—really stays there? Do you have a secret account or credit card you're hiding from your spouse? Are you calling all your doctors, friends, and doctor's friends in pain needing a few more pills? Have you been truthful about the motivation behind your decisions?

Hiding sin is almost always more dangerous than the sin itself. When we sin and then lie about it, we double our grievances, while continuing to act like everything is OK. Secrets keep things in the dark, and without the light of God's grace shining on those dark places, the secrets just fester and grow.

When we keep secrets, it's about image management, a gap between who we are and who we want others to think we are. When we keep secret sins, we care more about being thought of as spiritual, honorable, charitable, and so forth than actually being those things.

....

 Social media is a great experiment in painting a picture of who you want people to believe you are. Do you post the ups and downs of life, or do you portray a perfect image?

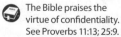 The Bible praises the virtue of confidentiality. See Proverbs 11:13; 25:9.

Nothing is wrong with being able to keep a secret, but some secrets aren't meant to be kept. Secrets that lead to duplicity, a compromised version of Christianity, and the loss of all we hold dear need to be revealed and renounced. God doesn't want us to be that kind of secret keeper. He wants us to live lives of integrity and openness that He can bless and that will bring us joy.

> "How happy is everyone who fears the LORD, who walks in His ways! You will surely eat what your hands have worked for. You will be happy, and it will go well for you. Your wife will be like a fruitful vine within your house, your sons, like young olive trees around your table. In this very way the man who fears the LORD will be blessed" (Psalm 128:1-4).

What does this passage promise for the person "who fears the LORD" and "walks in His ways"?

Nobody likes all the rules. As a matter of fact most of us hate rules and don't like being told what we can and cannot do. But God doesn't care if we like the rules; He just wants us to obey Him because His commandments bring holiness, happiness, and freedom.

Why are God's rules actually a means to freedom? When have you seen this to be true in your life?

What would happen right now if your private life were completely exposed? Would the fallout be extreme? In what ways might it be the best thing to happen to you?

LIVING IN TRUTH
Only God knows what Samson was capable of had he fully committed to following God's plan for His life. And the same is true for us. We all know we should be honest, but sometimes that's easier said than done. Let's look at two very practical ways we can keep our public and private lives pure.

Listen to "You Are" by Colton Dixon and "Life in Reverse" by The Wrecking from the *Samson* playlist, available at *threadsmedia.com/samson*.

1. Stay away from temptation.

I know you can handle it. I'm sure you won't give in. But few Christians I know started out wanting to throw away everything important to them.

Temptation is a slippery slope; a slow fade. Don't test yourself to see how strong you are and how close you can come to the edge. Instead, admit how weak you are and run away. A long look leads to a growing desire that hatches a crazy idea that culminates in a secret sin that leads to public pretending and hurt-filled lies.

Avoiding temptation altogether is the single most effective way to foil compromising situations that lead to lies and deception. But before you can avoid the temptation, you have to know where your temptation tendencies lie. If you can't spend, don't shop. If you don't want to lust, quit looking. If the doctor told you to watch your weight, stop going to the buffet and buying donuts. If you want to stop drinking, don't drop by the bar to see what your buddies are doing. If you don't want to end up crossing a line with your date, don't lay down on the couch or bed together.

We all have weaknesses that subtly draw us into a destructive pattern of sin.

>**"Each person is tempted when he is drawn away and enticed by his own evil desires. Then after desire has conceived, it gives birth to sin, and when sin is fully grown, it gives birth to death" (James 1:14-15).**

>**"Flee from youthful passions, and pursue righteousness, faith, love, and peace, along with those who call on the Lord from a pure heart" (2 Timothy 2:22).**

No matter your age, what "youthful passions" subtly tempt you? How can you avoid them? What needs to change?

Are those people, places, and things avoidable? If not, how can you guard your heart?

Once you've identified the things that easily persuade you from God's best, the next step is to cling to God and His Word:

....

 For more on what Scripture says about avoiding temptation, read Proverbs 2:11, Matthew 6:13; 26:40-41, Galatians 5:16, and James 4:7.

"No temptation has overtaken you except what is common to humanity. God is faithful, and He will not allow you to be tempted beyond what you are able, but with the temptation He will also provide a way of escape so that you are able to bear it" (1 Corinthians 10:13).

How can the promises in this passage help you focus on living out truth?

When we're giving all our attention to developing our relationship with God and concentrating on His ways, the appeal of our ungodly desires is greatly diminished. Temptation is real. It is going to happen. But you can prepare yourself by pinpointing those things that trip you up, and staying focused on the One who is stronger than any temptation we will encounter.

2. Get a friend.

Isolation aids secret sins. Samson had no friends to hold him accountable. Look again at Judges 14:

"His father went to visit the woman, and Samson prepared a feast there, as young men were accustomed to do. When the Philistines saw him, they brought 30 men to accompany him" (vv. 10-11).

Samson's parents brought the companions to his party, 30 of them to be exact. Of these companions, the best one of them, Samson's best man, ends up marrying Samson's wife (see Judges 15:1-2), as we'll see in the next session. That shows you how close they really were. Samson was a loaner. We don't read any mention of him having a close friend.

If Satan can get us alone, he's got us half beaten. If we want to get a leg up on the devil, we need to have authentic, God-honoring, trustworthy, call-us-out-when-we-do-wrong friends. Good friends are indispensable to a life of holiness.

In the Bible, Moses had Joshua (Deuteronomy 31; 34); Ruth had Naomi (Ruth 1–4); David had Jonathan (1 Samuel 20); Elijah had Elisha (1 Kings 19); and Paul had Barnabas (Acts 9; 13; 2 Timothy 4). In the fictional world, Tom Sawyer had Huck Finn. Gilligan had Skipper. Forrest had Bubba.

 Need a small group? Just grab a friend or two and begin walking together through prayer, confession, and Bible study. If you're not up for starting a guys group of your own, search for a Samson Society group in your area: *samsonsociety.net*.

What other examples of true friends have you seen?

Our ultimate example of the value of relationships is Christ Himself. Jesus had three: Peter, James, and John.

> **"Two are better than one because they have a good reward for their efforts. For if either falls, his companion can lift him up; but pity the one who falls without another to lift him up. Also, if two lie down together, they can keep warm; but how can one person alone keep warm? And if someone overpowers one person, two can resist him. A cord of three strands is not easily broken" (Ecclesiastes 4:9-12).**

We've talked about the importance of having a close friend. But maybe you don't have any. Or maybe the ones you have aren't good for your life. Instead of pointing you toward Jesus, they only distract you.

Friend or Foe?
We've all heard the clichés: "Bad company corrupts good morals." "Don't be unequally yoked to an unbeliever." "If you lie down with dogs, you get up with fleas." "Misery loves company." "You're known by the company you keep." These statements hold truth. Who we spend our time with affects who we become.

> **"The wounds of a friend are trustworthy, but the kisses of an enemy are excessive" (Proverbs 27:6).**

> **"Iron sharpens iron, and one man sharpens another" (Proverbs 27:17).**

Does the idea of having a friend like this make you feel excited or fearful? Why?

Some of my best friends have been made on the basketball court, the running trail, or on a hunting trip. Deep friendships grow out of time spent together. It's that time together that allows me to determine if I trust you or not.

 "When you have a problem, if you tell the truth, the problem becomes part of your past. If you lie, it becomes part of your future." —Rick Pitino, head coach of the University of Louisville men's basketball team[2]

When you find the right people, the chemistry is there, you "click" with them. Your personalities, sense of humor, goals, ambitions, and outlook on life mesh together. You have camaraderie. But most importantly, if the friendships look the way God intends, you have Christ-likeness. You inspire one another to godliness.

Who have you helped "sharpen"? Who helps sharpen you? How does it feel knowing you have their love and support?

Challenge yourself: Get in each others' grills. Somebody has to speak truth in love to you! Your life depends on it.

> **"But speaking the truth in love, let us grow in every way into Him who is the head—Christ. From Him the whole body, fitted and knit together by every supporting ligament, promotes the growth of the body for building up itself in love by the proper working of each individual part"** (Ephesians 4:15-16).

> **"Watch out, brothers, so that there won't be in any of you an evil, unbelieving heart that departs from the living God. But encourage each other daily, while it is still called today, so that none of you is hardened by sin's deception"** (Hebrews 3:12-13).

When we don't have friends who take care of and watch out for us, we run a greater risk of growing cold and calloused toward God. We need encouragement, and we need to give it, too. If we want to have good friends, we've got to be good friends.

Who have you encouraged today?

Who's your "Jonathan" or "Elisha"? Who is walking this life with you, encouraging you, correcting you, and pushing you toward Jesus?

Leading a group? Find extra questions and teaching tools in the leader kit, available for purchase at *threadsmedia.com/samson*.

If you can't honestly put any names in the space above, what small group, church, or event can you attend to begin finding and cultivating authentic friendships?

WHERE HEALING AND FORGIVENESS ARE FOUND

If you're going to have the depth of friendship that we're describing here, an element of active truth-telling must be involved. This develops trust like nothing else. Confessing our failures—both to God and to the people who can hold us accountable—is a necessary part of repentance and spiritual growth.

Samson kept his sin a secret. Then, as we'll later see, he made a joke about his secrets. Then his secrets made a joke out of him.

Secret sin grows. It becomes more convoluted and complicated. The best thing you can do is be real with God, with your close friends, with those you may have lied to, and then move forward.

So why do we need to confess our secrets?

Because God knows our secrets
We worship an omniscient God who knows all things, yet we fool ourselves into thinking He doesn't care or won't do anything about our secret sins.

> "You have set our unjust ways before You, our secret sins in the light of Your presence" (Psalm 90:8).

> "If we had forgotten the name of our God and spread out our hands to a foreign god, wouldn't God have found this out, since He knows the secrets of the heart?" (Psalm 44:20-21).

When have you tried to hide secrets from God? What was the result?

Because God will expose our secrets
Whether we like it or not, those secrets we think are hidden away, locked in a vault forever, will come screaming out eventually.

"There is nothing covered that won't be uncovered, nothing hidden that won't be made known. Therefore, whatever you have said in the dark will be heard in the light, and what you have whispered in an ear in private rooms will be proclaimed on the housetops" (Luke 12:2-3).

When have you personally experienced the consequences of deliberately disobeying God?

Because God will judge our secrets
This is one of those truths that should cause us to lose sleep at night when we're sleeping on our secrets.

"When all has been heard, the conclusion of the matter is: fear God and keep His commands, because this is for all humanity. For God will bring every act to judgment, including every hidden thing, whether good or evil" (Ecclesiastes 12:13-14).

The best thing you can do is confess your sin, repent, and turn toward integrity. The great news about confession is that we can be certain that when we confess, God is faithful to forgive—the very moment we ask. So do that right now.

Stop and pray, right where you are. Confess those sins you've held in secret.

What relief is felt when you admit your secrets to all-knowing God?

Because confession heals us
I've heard it said, "You are as sick as your secrets." Satan works in your secrets, using guilt as a power over you.

"Therefore, confess your sins to one another and pray for one another, so that you may be healed. The urgent request of a righteous person is very powerful in its effect" (James 5:16).

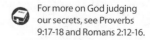

For more on God judging our secrets, see Proverbs 9:17-18 and Romans 2:12-16.

How can you pray for others in your life who need healing?

A guy who knew a thing or two about secrets and the sad consequences they bring was King David. He committed adultery, then to cover up the unintended pregnancy, he plotted a murder. But God knew and He sent the prophet Nathan to confront David. David confessed, but the prophet said there would be consequences to pay. And there were. David's family was divided, his kingdom was overthrown, and his child died.

> "When I kept silent, my bones became brittle from my groaning all day long. For day and night Your hand was heavy on me; my strength was drained as in the summer's heat. *Selah*. Then I acknowledged my sin to You and did not conceal my iniquity. I said, 'I will confess my transgressions to the LORD,' and You took away the guilt of my sin" (Psalm 32:3-5).

What have you learned from the secret keeping actions of Samson and even King David?

Go public with your good secrets, too! Samson seldom did. Had he been outspoken about his faith, his vow, and his purpose, I can't help but wonder if it would have provided a positive pressure for him to behave.

> "Therefore, everyone who will acknowledge Me before men, I will also acknowledge him before My Father in heaven. But whoever denies Me before men, I will also deny him before My Father in heaven" (Matthew 10:32-33).

What good things in your life—God's calling, the gifts He's given, the passions He's instilled—have you yet to share with the people you're closest to? How can you share your joy in the good things God's done in your life?

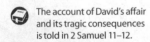
The account of David's affair and its tragic consequences is told in 2 Samuel 11–12.

Take a moment to encourage one other person in your life. What "good news" do you have for that person?

APPLY TO LIFE

> **CONNECT:** Maybe this lesson has been extraordinarily difficult because you don't have close friendships in your life before whom you can be open and honest. Pray that God would grant you these relationships. This week, start actively seeking them out.

> **STUDY:** Begin this week to study Samson's failures. In this lesson, we explored Samson's hidden secrets that destroyed him. Write down all of Samson's hidden secrets from Judges 14. Compare and contrast this with David's hidden secrets in 2 Samuel 11. Do you find anything that could point to some of your tendencies?

> **LISTEN:** Purchase "You Are" by Colton Dixon and "Life in Reverse" by The Wrecking (see the playlist at *threadsmedia.com/samson*). Add these to your regular mix of music throughout the week so that you'll be reminded of the truth of God's Word.

ENERGY
REFOCUSED

Don't control your anger.

3

Everybody deals with anger. In a world of frustrations, pain, sin, and missed opportunities, anger is a given. So the question isn't so much "Are you angry?" but "How do you deal with your anger?" Most people express their anger in unhealthy ways. The Federal Bureau of Investigation says that a violent crime occurs every 24 seconds, an aggravated assault every 48 seconds, and a murder every 23 minutes. Domestic violence is the leading cause of ER visits by women, and 1,500 people a year are killed or injured in incidents of road rage.

As we'll see throughout this session, Samson was often consumed by anger. The glory of God was the furthest thing from his mind. Samson's anger began with and ended with himself, and a lot of people were hurt and even killed in the process. Yet God used him in spite of—and even through—his fury.

Samson's experience teaches us that if we want to maximize our lives, we've got to learn to deal with our tempers in a God-honoring way. Through the next part of Samson's story, we'll learn about the destructiveness of anger, how it progresses, and how to overcome this consuming emotion.

ANGER IS A PIGGY-BACK EMOTION

We learned in the first session that Samson demanded his parents go get a Philistine woman he had seen and wanted to marry. Here we find Samson at his rehearsal dinner. In a drunken and arrogant moment, he offered a bet to the Philistine men.

Samson's wager came in the form of a riddle originating from his encounter with the honey inside the lion's carcass (Judges 14:8-9). Again we see Samson's deception and pride corrupting his judgment and provoking his eventual outrage and revenge.

> "'Let me tell you a riddle,' Samson said to them. 'If you can explain it to me during the seven days of the feast and figure it out, I will give you 30 linen garments and 30 changes of clothes. But if you can't explain it to me, you must give me 30 linen garments and 30 changes of clothes.' 'Tell us your riddle,' they replied. 'Let's hear it.' So he said to them: *Out of the eater came something to eat, and out of the strong came something sweet.* After three days, they were unable to explain the riddle" (Judges 14:12-14, emphasis mine).

The Philistine men tried for days to figure out Samson's riddle, but they never could. Finally they found Samson's fiancée and threatened her life to force her to help them find out the riddle's answer.

 Watch the *Samson* video for Session 3,
available at *threadsmedia.com/samson*.

"On the fourth day they said to Samson's wife, 'Persuade your husband to explain the riddle to us, or we will burn you and your father's household to death. Did you invite us here to rob us?' So Samson's wife came to him, weeping, and said, 'You hate me and don't love me! You told my people the riddle, but haven't explained it to me.' 'Look,' he said, 'I haven't even explained it to my father or mother, so why should I explain it to you?'" (vv. 15-16).

Samson resisted her questions initially, but as her tears intensified and his honeymoon drew near, he caved in and told her.

"She wept the whole seven days of the feast, and at last, on the seventh day, he explained it to her, because she had nagged him so much. Then she explained it to her people" (v. 17).

Samson's unnamed fiancée revealed his secret to her kinsmen and, just under the deadline, the Philistines solved Samson's riddle.

"On the seventh day, before sunset, the men of the city said to him: What is sweeter than honey? What is stronger than a lion?

So he said to them: If you hadn't plowed with my young cow, you wouldn't know my riddle now!

The Spirit of the LORD took control of him, and he went down to Ashkelon and killed 30 of their men. He stripped them and gave their clothes to those who had explained the riddle. In a rage, Samson returned to his father's house, and his wife was given to one of the men who had accompanied him" (Judges 14:18-20).

Samson's anger burned. Literally translated, it was "set on fire." Have you ever felt like that, when your nostrils flare, your face turns read, and your breathing becomes shallow and intense? It's hard to make rational decisions when you're that enraged.

The scene is easy to imagine: Samson stomped down to a nearby Philistine city and slaughtered 30 innocent men. He returned and threw down the clothes of his victims as payment of his debt, storming back to his house and stewing every step.

What do you think really fueled Samson's anger in this story?

 Thomas Jefferson believed that when you're angry you should count to 10. When you're very angry, count to 100.

What things tend to set your anger off? Are there certain events? certain people?

Samson was mad that the Philistines found a way to solve his riddle, but more than likely, he was embarrassed that his fiancée's betrayal made him look like a fool. He had been all brash and bad, but then he got had.

When we get irate, it's most often because someone else has done something to offend us—like cutting us off in traffic, saying something derogatory about our momma, or discovering a friend shared a secret she shouldn't have. Our haphazard response? We get mad and lose our temper. Then almost simultaneously, we feel stressed, embarrassed, and ashamed at our behavior—or at least we should.

I'm guilty of this, too. Here's one example: I recently lost my temper with the three girls in my house. My daughters are deathly afraid of wasps, freaking out when one is around. We were at a hunting camp cleaning up, and a wasp was on the refrigerator. My oldest daughter lost her nerves and muttered hysterically, "Daddy, there's a wasp!" I wanted to say, "Well, honey, kill it." But you know only daddy's can kill wasps. I found myself getting frustrated with her. My thoughts raced, *Why do I have to kill the wasp? Why can't you?* Why did I feel that way? It's simple: I didn't want to stop what I was doing. It was an interruption I didn't want to deal with.

Later that same day, when we had reached our deer stand, I checked it for wasps before the girls got in. I found one, got it out, and climbed down. When my daughter climbed in, she found another one: "Daddy there's a wasp!" she yelled. So I had to climb back up to get the wasp out. I was mad. Why? Because again I was delayed in getting to do what I wanted to do.

It gets worse. After the hunt, my family was standing around with some other hunters when my wife announced: "We saw a good buck in our stand!" I just about flipped out on her and had to explain one of the basic rules of hunting. You never tell another hunter where you saw a good deer! I found myself for the third time in the same day getting angry at my family. Why? Because I'm selfish. I only wanted *my* family to kill the big bucks.

When our anger and frustration subside, the ramifications of our actions are often worse than the thing that set us off to begin with. That's definitely how I felt that day.

 If you struggle with anger management, consider more study. Check out Gary Chapman's book *Anger: Handling a Powerful Emotion in a Healthy Way*.

When have you seen this to be true in your life?

How do you usually feel after you lose your temper?

THE ANGER THIEF

We say stuff when we're mad that we don't necessarily mean but can never take back. We aim to wound, but that wound can't be undone. It's irreversible.

Eventually, Samson's anger subsided and he decided to go visit his wife to patch things up. But Judges 15 tells us that her father didn't let him see her. He thought Samson hated her, so he had given her to Samson's best man.

> **"Later on, during the wheat harvest, Samson took a young goat as a gift and visited his wife. 'I want to go to my wife in her room,' he said. But her father would not let him enter. 'I was sure you hated her,' her father said, 'so I gave her to one of the men who accompanied you. Isn't her younger sister more beautiful than she is? Why not take her instead?'" (Judges 15:1-2).**

What did Samson say in his fit of rage that made his father-in-law think he hated his daughter intensely?

Samson's father-in-law apparently thought the relationship was over, based on Samson's actions. He gave Samson's wife to another man in order to save his daughter's dignity, since Samson abandoned her at the altar. Anger cost Samson his girl. It's worth noting that verse 2 shows that the girl's father took some responsibility for what happened at the wedding. He attempted to patch things up with Samson, offering a compromise in the form of his younger daughter's hand in marriage. Given her beauty, this seems like an impressive offer, but Samson's pride and determination to make his own choices caused him to reject the would-be bride. This makes it even more clear that Samson didn't find fault within himself for leaving the wedding in a rage. Apparently, he expected to return as though nothing had happened and continue life with his bride.

Anger doesn't work that way. Outbursts of rage cannot be undone.

 Listen to "Lose Myself" by tobyMac and "Only a Mountain" by Jason Castro from the *Samson* playlist, available at *threadsmedia.com/samson*.

The same is true in our own lives. We may think anger is a good idea because it makes us feel good or it makes others fear us. Sometimes we use anger to control others and get what we want—by scaring our kids into behaving or convincing a nagging wife to leave us alone. We intimidate our employees into being more productive. Or maybe we like knowing that people give us our way just to keep us from blowing up. But none of these reactions are how God has called us to behave when things don't go our way. In the end, anger always robs us.

> "A fool gives full vent to his anger, but a wise man holds it in check" (Proverbs 29:11).

How have you seen people use anger against you? Did their tactics work? How did their tactics change the nature of your relationship?

Giving in to our inflamed emotions makes us more than fools. It's outright dangerous—a gateway emotion that leads to stronger and more powerful explosions with each person or thing that sets us off. Jesus addressed the problems of murder and anger (among others) in Matthew 5.

> "You have heard that it was said to our ancestors, Do not murder, and whoever murders will be subject to judgment. But I tell you, everyone who is angry with his brother will be subject to judgment" (vv. 21-22).

Jesus explained that obedience to God's commands means not having murderous hearts as well as not having murderous hands. We're called to respond to personal offenses with forbearance and forgiveness rather than with anger and violence. That makes biblical obedience regarding our anger a lot tougher, because it requires both physical and emotional restraint.

— Why do you think Jesus equates anger with murder? Is that too big of a leap? Why or why not?

— Which do you find more difficult to obey—the physical or emotional restraint of your anger? Explain.

 "Don't let your spirit rush to be angry, for anger abides in the heart of fools" (Ecclesiastes 7:9).

Read Romans 5:6-11. How does God's treatment of us, according to these verses, compare with how He expects us to treat others, according to Matthew 5:43-44?

Mark Atteberry, in his book *The Samson Syndrome,* suggests that anger is addictive. It's like a drug that gives us an adrenaline rush or a sense of invincibility. When we see other people jump into action (or stand down) when we "go off," we like it. It makes us feel like the big dog or the tough guy on campus. Like a drug addict defined by addiction, anger can easily become our identity.

A friend of mine said he was at an 11-year-olds football game when he witnessed an explosion of anger. The offensive team ran a sweep around the end and the young man playing the cornerback position on defense missed a tackle that allowed the opposing team to score. The child's dad was on the sidelines and immediately threw down his hat and started cursing. As his child ran to the sideline, he called him over and started yelling at him and pointing into the kid's chest, giving him a piece of his mind. Steve said the kid was looking up at his dad in disbelief, with those "what in the world are you doing?" eyes. Then he pushed his child toward his team on the sideline.

How did the father's reaction make him feel? his child? bystanders? What long-term ramifications did it likely have on the father/son relationship?

Has anger ever cost you anything? Was that "thing" it cost you recoverable or forever lost?

Anger's Deception
Samson paid the price of the dowry, and he was left with neither his money nor his girl. He had been "done wrong." But he was about to hurt innocent people again because anger blinded his thought-process.

> "Samson said to them, 'This time I won't be responsible when I harm the Philistines.' So he went out and caught 300 foxes. He took torches, turned the foxes tail-to-tail, and put a torch between each pair of tails. Then he ignited the torches and released the foxes into the standing grain of the Philistines. He burned up the piles of grain and the standing grain as well

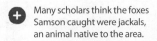

Many scholars think the foxes Samson caught were jackals, an animal native to the area.

as the vineyards and olive groves. Then the Philistines asked, 'Who did this?' They were told, 'It was Samson, the Timnite's son-in-law, because he has taken Samson's wife and given her to another man.' So the Philistines went to her and her father and burned them to death" (Judges 15:3-6).

Samson had a "scorched earth" policy when it came to getting even. He made people pay, and he felt no remorse.

What surprises you most about Samson's reaction?

What examples of blinding anger have you heard about or experienced personally? What was the result?

In anger, we justify ourselves and our actions, regardless of how over-the-top they are. But in reality, this type of blinding anger turns our world upside-down. We set out to prove ourselves right and avenge what was done to us; we lash out in anger to make ourselves feel in control, "like a man." Yet the result is often disastrous, compounding the problems we started with, and destroying the relationships—and possibly lives—of those around us.

> **"An angry man stirs up conflict, and a hot-tempered man increases rebellion" (Proverbs 29:22).**

It takes more strength to subdue ourselves than it does to explode emotionally, verbally, or physically on others. Having the wherewithal to maintain patience and peace in difficult situations is a sign of maturity and godliness.

Read Proverbs 16:32. Think back over the last year or so. Do your actions display that you believe the truth of this verse? What areas of your life might need to be tweaked in light of this truth?

How does restraint show strength? When have you seen this proven true in your life?

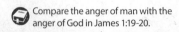 Compare the anger of man with the anger of God in James 1:19-20.

You may feel like "the man" when you go off and people jump up. But the Bible says you become "the man" when you control your temper and overlook a transgression.

> **"A person's insight gives him patience, and his virtue is to overlook an offense" (Proverbs 19:11).**

A person full of restraint and grace is a person of great strength.

Anger Escalates

When the Philistines discovered who torched their economy, they took revenge upon themselves. They couldn't find Samson, so they killed his wife and her father. In classic Samson fashion, he retaliated, this time by slaughtering people.

> **"Then Samson told them, 'Because you did this, I swear that I won't rest until I have taken vengeance on you.' He tore them limb from limb with a great slaughter, and he went down and stayed in the cave at the rock of Etam" (Judges 15:7-8).**

We've gone from a harmless riddle to a ruthless rampage. We've escalated from a misunderstanding to destruction of crops and houses. Now we arrive at the destruction of human life. Samson acts out of revenge yet again, failing to see that his escalating cycle of violence will not end with another destructive action:

> **"The Philistines went up, camped in Judah, and raided Lehi. So the men of Judah said, 'Why have you attacked us?' They replied, 'We have come to arrest Samson and pay him back for what he did to us.' Then 3,000 men of Judah went to the cave at the rock of Etam, and they asked Samson, 'Don't you realize that the Philistines rule over us? What have you done to us?' 'I have done to them what they did to me,' he answered. They said to him, 'We've come to arrest you and hand you over to the Philistines.' Then Samson told them, 'Swear to me that you yourselves won't kill me.' 'No,' they said, 'we won't kill you, but we will tie you up securely and hand you over to them.' So they tied him up with two new ropes and led him away from the rock. When he came to Lehi, the Philistines came to meet him shouting. The Spirit of the LORD took control of him, and the ropes that were on his arms became like burnt flax and his bonds fell off his wrists. He found a fresh jawbone of a donkey, reached out his hand, took it, and killed 1,000 men with it" (Judges 15:9-15).**

 Human revenge against an enemy is demonstrated in many circumstances in the Old Testament: Genesis 4:23-24; Judges 20:10; Proverbs 6:32-34; 1 Samuel 18:25; and Ezekiel 25:12-17.

Samson's ironic reply in verse 11 tells the story of this chapter: "I have done to them what they did to me." Revenge is an uncontrollable monster. Each act of retaliation brings another. It's a boomerang that cannot be thrown without cost to the thrower. In this story, words like "avenge," "take vengeance," and "repay" pop off the page. Anger, violence, and retaliation, once set in motion, are incredibly hard to stop.

Even if the other person doesn't retaliate, anger has to intensify in order to keep getting the desired result. Screaming and shouting and raising your voice works for a while, but then you have to take it up a notch. You have to start throwing things, slamming stuff, hitting walls, and hitting people.

When have you experienced intensifying anger and vengeance? What was the result? How did you overcome the situation?

Anger isn't always a bad thing, however. There's a healthy kind of anger that the Bible calls "righteous anger." In Scripture, anger caused Jesus to cleanse the temple (John 2:13-22). The apostle Paul was beside himself because the Galatians had returned to the Law after it was abolished through Christ (Galatians 1:6-10). Even God Himself burns with righteous indignation at sin:

> **"God is a righteous judge and a God who shows His wrath every day" (Psalm 7:11).**

How does it make you feel that God is righteous and an avenger of wrongs?

In our lives, anger can energize us as we grow sick of being in debt, sick of being an addict, or angry about being overweight. Anger at a common cause, like child abuse or terrorism, can unite people to affect change and improve life situations or prevent victimization. In short, righteous anger can motivate us to improve, grow, and strengthen ourselves and our relationships.

But most anger isn't healthy, righteous, or energizing. Eleanor Roosevelt said, "Anger is only one letter short of danger."[1] Author Wayne Dyer, in his book *Your Erroneous Zones*, said "anger is an erroneous zone, a kind of psychological influenza that incapacitates you

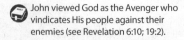
John viewed God as the Avenger who vindicates His people against their enemies (see Revelation 6:10; 19:2).

just as a physical disease would. . . . Anger is a choice, as well as a habit. It is a learned reaction to frustration, in which you behave in ways that you would rather not. In fact, severe anger is a form of insanity."[2]

Most of us don't deal with anger very well, but mark my words: How you deal with anger matters to God.

How do you define the difference between "righteous anger" and "unrighteous anger"?

When you get angry, is it typically righteous or detrimental? How can you tell?

Which is most often the case for you—anger blinding or escalating? What are some ways you've learned to control it?

OVERCOMING ANGER

Samson's life proves that he didn't have a good handle on his emotions. He could have benefitted from the wise words of the apostle Paul, who talked about laying aside the "old self" and putting on a "new self" in Jesus (Ephesians 4). While it's too late for Samson, it's not to late for us to model godly self-control in the face of difficult times and circumstances.

Paul's insight into overcoming anger is priceless for those of us who struggle in this area. (Hint: We *all* do at some point.)

1. Refuse to Stew.

You've heard it said that "sticks and stones may break my bones, but words will never hurt me." Paul would heartily disagree with that adage. The truth is words are powerful, and they can either build others up or tear them down. And our culture doesn't always promote language that encourages and edifies. The Bible tells us that anger is not only OK, it's expected. But we are to have control of our tempers, to get mad when anger is warranted:

> **"Be angry and do not sin. Don't let the sun go down on your anger . . . "**
> **(Ephesians 4:26).**

 "And the tongue is a fire. The tongue, a world of unrighteousness, is placed among the parts of our bodies. It pollutes the whole body, sets the course of life on fire, and is set on fire by hell" (James 3:6).

 80 percent of rapists motivated with displaced anger come from fatherless homes.[3]

Paul recognized that we all experience situations that spark the emotion of anger. Believers who became incensed or irritated with other Christians were to resolve the conflict before the sun set. That is, they were to deal with the issue squarely and quickly rather than let it simmer and become divisive. Unresolved differences destroy relationships. We mustn't wait to settle a dispute with another Christian.

So what does that look like on a daily basis? When you get mad, stop and ask what the issue is at its core. *Is my anger righteous and healthy, or is my anger piggy backing on my own feelings of selfishness, stress, or a desire for power? Is the problem me or them? Am I defending myself or God?* Then you have to talk about your anger. Don't just sweep stuff under the rug, because soon enough it comes out. Or it becomes a massive mountain in the middle of the room and, like a volcano, erupts violently.

A lot of times anger grows in the absence of information. You aren't communicating with the people you are at odds with, so you start making up the story in your mind. Don't do that. Go talk to the person you're angry with and ask for clarification. Find a way to express how it makes you feel and what is going on within you. Refuse to stew. Have a conversation with God, with yourself, and with others.

How do you respond to this verse? Is it really possible to be angry and not sin? Explain.

Describe a time when you or someone you know allowed anger to boil under the surface? What did you learn from that experience?

2. Recognize Anger as a Spiritual Attack.
Anger is a spiritual attack. When we allow anger to enter our hearts and minds, we no longer have complete control. The Devil can get a foothold in our lives and in our relationships.

> **" . . . and don't give the Devil an opportunity" (Ephesians 4:27).**

When the Devil gets a foothold, he will cause a root of bitterness to grow up, poisoning your whole life. He wants to sabotage your actions and purpose, your efforts to live obediently and wholeheartedly to God.

The first mention of anger in the Bible is Genesis 4, when Cain got angry and killed his brother. God asked Cain why he was angry.

 If you're a parent, modeling healthy anger is essential for your child's emotional development. Learn more by reading "Achieve positive goals through healthy anger" by Gary Oliver, Ph.D. at *lifeway.com.*

"And Abel also presented an offering—some of the firstborn of his flock and their fat portions. The LORD had regard for Abel and his offering, but He did not have regard for Cain and his offering. Cain was furious, and he looked despondent. Then the LORD said to Cain, 'Why are you furious? And why do you look despondent? If you do what is right, won't you be accepted? But if you do not do what is right, sin is crouching at the door. Its desire is for you, but you must rule over it'" (Genesis 4:4-7).

You must learn to master your anger. You can't do it in your own strength. The Holy Spirit will help you master sin. It will be a lifelong battle and won't be over until you see Jesus. But you can win.

But what about the flip side, righteous wrath? All believers should be opposed to evil but the problem is when we assume justification for our response to that evil. Righteous wrath can degenerate into resentment or frustration to the point that it becomes sin. If we don't control wrath, it can take the form of flashes of temper toward others. What should be constructive anger can easily flame out of control. When that happens, believers give the Devil an opportunity, and evil gains a foothold in individual believers and in the Christian community.

Do you believe anger opens the door to the Devil's devastation in our lives? What supports your answer?

Besides anger, what other attitudes give the Devil a foothold in your life?

3. Rely on the Holy Spirit.
Paul strongly urged believers not to grieve the Holy Spirit. His injunction reminded Christians of God's presence.

> **"And don't grieve God's Holy Spirit. You were sealed by Him for the day of redemption" (Ephesians 4:30).**

You have a secret weapon: prayer! When you're struggling to control your anger—or any emotional or physical response for that matter—ask the Spirit to help you and to rule you. When you see a bad situation coming or feel stressed, call on the Holy Spirit to help. Draw near to God and Satan has to flee (see James 4:7-8).

 Leading a group? Find extra questions and teaching tools in the leader kit, available for purchase at *threadsmedia.com/samson.*

When have you felt the Holy Spirit work in your life previously? How can that work reassure you that the Spirit can help you in the present and in the future?

How can He help you seek God's best for your life when you're feeling righteously or unrighteously angry?

4. Remember the Costs of Your Actions.
The most common way we harm others as a result of our anger is through the poor use of our speech.

> **"No foul language is to come from your mouth, but only what is good for building up someone in need, so that it gives grace to those who hear" (Ephesians 4:29).**

Take time to calm down before you choose how to respond. Seek to be compassionate, patient, and gentle with others. We all mess up and anger others. React to those who make you mad in the way you want those you make mad to react to you. Rotten words are destructive, hurtful, and they cannot be taken back. Life and death are found in the power of your tongue, so set a guard over your mouth.

What's the most difficult thing about controlling your tongue? How can you give that over to God's vindication?

5. Realign Your Heart to God.
We're called to be kind in our interactions with others. To be kind is to consider others' good as important as our own. We're to be compassionate—to extend heart-felt empathy concerning others' needs. We're to feel with others in their distress and help if possible. Even Christians sometimes wrong one another, but as God graciously provided forgiveness through Christ's atoning death, we are to keep on forgiving one another.

> **"All bitterness, anger and wrath, shouting and slander must be removed from you, along with all malice. And be kind and compassionate to one another, forgiving one another, just as God also forgave you in Christ" (Ephesians 4:31-32).**

 "A hot-tempered man stirs up conflict, but a man slow to anger calms strife" (Proverbs 15:18).

The Greek word behind *forgiving* is not the usual word for forgive. It has the idea of graciousness toward others and includes pardoning wrongs. God's gracious forgiveness is to be the model and motive for believers' extending forgiveness. Because God has forgiven us, we must forgive others. The revenge cycle can only be halted by forgiveness.

When just one believer lives by Paul's commands in these verses, that person has a positive impact on the church's life and can move others to live by these principles. Will you be that one person?

Let it go and give it to God. How? Offer forgiveness. You have to let God change your identity. My prayer is that you'd let God transform you today. Unresolved differences destroy relationships. Because God has forgiven you, you're called to forgive others. When you forgive others for hurtful words, wrong attitudes, and immoral actions, you foster an environment in which real community can exist.

The world is watching your reaction to frustrations and inconveniences. How will you respond?

APPLY TO LIFE

> **PRAY:** During your time with God this week, ask Him to reveal times in your life when you've been blind to your own impatience and anger. When He does, confess those sins.

> **OBSERVE:** As you watch TV and interact with people this week, take note of the different things that set people off in anger. Then note what it takes for them to actually move through that and arrive on the other side. Anything pointing back to the truth of Scripture?

> **STUDY:** Study the anger of Jesus this week (Matthew 21:12-17,23-27; Mark 11:15-19,27-33; Luke 19:45-48; 20:1-8). Dig deep into the story, looking for the motivation behind His growing anger. Search your own heart, and see if the things that got Jesus fired up get you fired up as well.

> **LISTEN:** Purchase "Lose Myself" by tobyMac and "Only a Mountain" by Jason Castro (see the playlist at *threadsmedia.com/samson*). Add these to your regular mix of music throughout the week to focus your energy on honoring God.

GROWTH
UNCOMPROMISED

Don't cultivate your spiritual life.

4

Marcus Dupree, whose story was told on ESPN's film documentary *30 for 30,* was a high school football phenomenon. He broke every scoring record, becoming a hometown hero and a Mississippi legend. His recruitment garnered a book, *The Courting of Marcus Dupree.* He had every college coach in America coming to his house. The University of Texas and Oklahoma even sent recruiters to live in Philadelphia, Mississippi, to monitor his every move. Everybody wanted this kid. His freshman year at Oklahoma, Dupree turned college football upside down. He was unstoppable. His sophomore year he was the favorite to win the Heisman trophy. Dupree graced the cover of *Sports Illustrated* on a fast track to the NFL. His yellow jacket for the Hall of Fame was already being fitted. Marcus Dupree couldn't miss. But the story sadly turned south. Literally.

After a rift with his college coach, questionable advice from family friends, and a hard hit on the football field, Dupree's life began to unravel. He left the national spotlight to enroll in Division 1 college football at the University of Southern Mississippi. But he never saw the football field again in college.

In desperation, Dupree bluffed his way into a contract with the upstart United States Football League's New Orleans Breakers. In his second game, he suffered a knee injury that ended any hopes of greatness. His million dollar contract disappeared like a vapor in the wind. The media quit covering him, and the world of football moved on. ESPN called this story, "The Greatest That Never Was." I watched Dupree's story in disbelief, wondering what could have been.[1]

WASTED POTENTIAL

We see wasted potential all the time. In the classroom, there are kids with bright minds, incredible intelligence quotients, and unbelievable creative abilities. They waste their potential by not devoting themselves to studying and developing their raw resources. Instead of applying themselves with diligence, they opt for the easy road of "just getting by."

We see wasted potential in the corporate world, too. A young person leaves college with charisma, charm, and competence, but he doesn't want to work and pay his dues. He'd rather rely on charm and good looks, trusting that success will just fall into his lap because of who he is. Soon his peers pass him by. He changes jobs, and then careers, thinking that he got into the wrong field. But laziness and a poor work ethic don't discriminate career fields. He ends up frustrated, never achieving what was once possible.

 Watch the *Samson* video for Session 4, available at *threadsmedia.com/samson.*

 The NFL Players Association says of the 9,000 college football players, the NFL invites just 310 to its scouting combine every year. Most of them will not make it onto an NFL roster.[2]

People also waste spiritual potential. God has an incredible plan for each of our lives. But without due diligence and discipline in cultivating a heart for God, those plans never come to pass. Great potential is wasted because our character and devotion to God aren't equal to the great things He has planned.

When you were a kid, who/what did you want to be when you grew up?

If you haven't achieved that, what has stopped you? How much does a lack of potential or wasted potential play into your story?

Samson was a kid with so much potential. In this session, we're going to see him in his finest hour, a glimpse of what could have been.

SAMSON'S STORY

Judges 15 reveals the first time Samson acted unselfishly. After spiraling back and forth in acts of vengeance with the Philistines, Samson finally withdrew and went without a fight. Let's recap a little from last session. Read verses 9-13 again.

> **"The Philistines went up, camped in Judah, and raided Lehi. So the men of Judah said, 'Why have you attacked us?' They replied, 'We have come to arrest Samson and pay him back for what he did to us.' Then 3,000 men of Judah went to the cave at the rock of Etam, and they asked Samson, 'Don't you realize that the Philistines rule over us? What have you done to us?' 'I have done to them what they did to me,' he answered. They said to him, 'We've come to arrest you and hand you over to the Philistines.' Then Samson told them, 'Swear to me that you yourselves won't kill me.' 'No,' they said, 'we won't kill you, but we will tie you up securely and hand you over to them.' So they tied him up with two new ropes and led him away from the rock."**

Is a person set on revenge ever "right"? Explain your response.

 In the ancient Near East, "cities of refuge" were set up to avert endless cycles of revenge (see Joshua 20).

Who seems to be Israel's biggest enemy at this point—the Philistines or Samson? Why might Samson have been so calm when he surrendered to the Philistines?

The Philistine army had threatened that they would kill Israelites and bring suffering to the people until Samson responded. So once Samson became aware of the threat to God's people, he willingly surrendered and consented to go without a fight. This whole act required faith. For him to walk down into the camp of the enemy bound by ropes meant that his life was in danger. But Samson trusted God to deliver him.

As Samson walked into the enemy camp, a war cry rose up from the bad guys. Finally they would rid themselves of this renegade—or so they thought. The shouts of the enemy were meant to intimidate, but the taunts of these soldiers only served to provoke the Spirit of God to rise up and rush over Samson.

> **"When he came to Lehi, the Philistines came to meet him shouting. The Spirit of the LORD took control of him, and the ropes that were on his arms became like burnt flax and his bonds fell off his wrists. He found a fresh jawbone of a donkey, reached out his hand, took it, and killed 1,000 men with it" (Judges 15:14-15).**

When else have you seen "the Spirit of the Lord" take control of a person?

What was the result? What can you infer about the situation when this happens?

In an incredible scene, like one from a superhero movie, Samson broke the cords that restrained his body. Anointed by the Holy Spirit, Samson, grabbed the only weapon within his reach—the jawbone of a dead donkey. He unleashed the fire of the Lord against them. There's no doubt that danger rushed at Samson from every direction, but with every enemy attack, the Spirit of the Lord supplied new strength and protection. When the fury subsided, Samson stood unharmed. Around him lay the bodies and blood of 1,000 Philistine fighters.

 During the period of the Judges, the Spirit of the Lord came to individuals and empowered them to accomplish specific tasks (Judges 3:10; 6:34; 11:29; 13:25; 14:6; 14:19).

Following his victory, Samson penned a poem celebrating his triumph:

> **"With the jawbone of a donkey I have piled them in a heap. With the jawbone of a donkey I have killed 1,000 men" (Judges 15:16).**

But the celebration didn't last long. God reminded Samson that he was just a man. His spiritual and emotional tank bottomed out, and physically Samson was running on fumes. In weakness, he cried out to God.

> **"When he finished speaking, he threw away the jawbone and named that place Ramath-lehi. He became very thirsty and called out to the LORD: 'You have accomplished this great victory through Your servant. Must I now die of thirst and fall into the hands of the uncircumcised?' So God split a hollow place in the ground at Lehi, and water came out of it. After Samson drank, his strength returned, and he revived. That is why he named it En-hakkore, which is in Lehi to this day" (Judges 15:17-19).**

What surprises you more about this passage—that Samson recognized God's provision, that God answered Samson's prayer, or that God answered the prayer in such a phenomenal way? Why?

As God did for the Israelites in the wilderness, He miraculously provided water from the hollow place, a bowl-shaped spot on the limestone ground. Where before there had been no spring, now there flowed a fresh, life-giving river of water. Samson drank and felt renewed. Yet God did more than answer his prayer for water. He established Samson as the judge over Israel.

> **"And he judged Israel 20 years in the days of the Philistines" (Judges 15:20).**

What does Samson's long tenure in office tell us about his relationship with God during this period?

We have no details of Samson's tenure in leadership. A 20-year gap of silence falls between Judges 15 and 16. One could argue this implies that Samson was an effective leader for that period of time. Or, it can be easily argued that Samson remained

---

 Does your Bible translation have "LORD" in verse 18 written in all caps? That indicates that Samson called on God, the covenant God of Israel, the name God spoke to Moses in the wilderness: YHWH.

 En-hakkore means "the spring of the caller" or "the spring of the namer."

self-centered. Regardless, God continued to work through Samson to accomplish His will—to begin to remove the Israelites from Philistine rule. Samson may have had different plans for his life, but God's will was accomplished.

✶ "Many plans are in a man's heart, but the LORD's decree will prevail" (Proverbs 19:21).

— What does it tell us about God that He worked through someone as imperfect as Samson?

— How does this verse affect the way you view your decisions? your life purpose?

SAMSON'S UNREACHED POTENTIAL

Despite Samson's many faults, his victory is evidence of what could have been possible when he depended on God to guide and sustain him. Let's examine the elements that helped make him successful.

1. Samson prayed.

For the first time in the whole story, Samson acknowledged God and his need of divine help. He called out to God, and God answered the prayer. Miraculously, water appeared from a rock in the desert. All Samson had to do was call on God, and the Creator of the world was ready, willing, and able to answer.

He'll do the same for us. Sometimes it feels selfish to ask God to do something for us, to work in our lives and guide us through a difficult situation or task. But the Bible tells us that God wants us to take our concerns to Him. It's part of the relationship we have with the Father.

"He did not even spare His own Son but offered Him up for us all; how will He not also with Him grant us everything?" (Romans 8:32).

"Don't worry about anything, but in everything, through prayer and petition with thanksgiving, let your requests be made known to God. And the peace of God, which surpasses every thought, will guard your hearts and minds in Christ Jesus" (Philippians 4:6-7).

 Normally an announcement of how many years a judge served appears at the end of his or her story. In Samson's case, another chapter follows in which Samson operates on his own strength once again.

Have you ever been hesitant to ask God for something because it felt selfish? What did you do?

How do you know whether your prayers are selfish or God-honoring?

Does praying for ourselves mean God will always grant our requests? Why or why not?

2. Samson revealed his understanding of his covenant with God.
The Bible says that Samson called on Yahweh, the covenant God of Israel. Samson's recognition of his covenant with God allowed him to strip the glory from the Philistines' false god—giving ultimate honor and glory to God.

Today, because of Jesus' work on the cross, we are under God's covenant of grace (see Hebrews 8). Because of this covenant relationship, we know that God has a plan and a purpose to use each of us to bring glory to His name and advance His kingdom.

How can you bring honor and glory to God where you are right now?

3. Samson acknowledged God's sovereignty.
Samson knew that his great power and victory were from God. He knew who he was and what his life was supposed to be about. Basically, Samson recognized that God brought about the deliverance of the Israelites (and himself) from Philistine control. He affirmed that God had given him the strength and ability to win. Samson acknowledged God's sovereign rule and control, similar to Paul's declaration in 1 Timothy 6:

> "He is the blessed and only Sovereign, the King of kings, and the Lord of lords, the only One who has immortality, dwelling in unapproachable light; no one has seen or can see Him, to Him be honor and eternal might" (vv. 15b-16).

 Listen to "Hope for Us All" by Je'kob, "One Thing Remains" by Passion, and "Wake Up" by All Sons & Daughters from the *Samson* playlist, available at *threadsmedia.com/samson*.

 "Being a Christian is less about cautiously avoiding sin than about courageously and actively doing God's will." —Dietrich Bonhoeffer[3]

What does it look like to acknowledge God's power and control in our lives today?

4. Samson, even for a moment, saw himself rightly.
After the Philistine battle, Samson acknowledged himself as God's "servant" (v. 18). Like Abraham, Isaac, Jacob, Moses, Joshua, Caleb, Job, and David, he was a servant of God. Samson had a streak of egomania, to say the least, but for once he got it right.

Samson's fatal flaw, what likely contributed to his ultimate demise, was his craving for self-glorification. Pride is a killer of potential. Paul described how pride affects our desire to honor God in Romans 7:

> **"For in my inner self I joyfully agree with God's law. But I see a different law in the parts of my body, waging war against the law of my mind and taking me prisoner to the law of sin in the parts of my body. What a wretched man I am! Who will rescue me from this dying body?" (Romans 7:22-24).**

In what ways can pride derail you from fulfilling your God-given potential?

When has pride clouded your judgment? What was the result?

What can you do to keep pride in check?

UNDISCIPLINED LIVING
One of the most haunting questions for Samson—and for our own lives—is the question, "What if?" *What if Samson's entire life had been marked by those four realities: prayer, intimacy with God, trust in the Sovereign, and humility in the midst of fulfilling God's purpose? What if he had prayed more? What if he had maintained intimacy with the covenant God? What if he had trusted God's sovereignty completely? What if he had given himself wholeheartedly to being God's servant?*

Sadly, we will never know because that isn't what happened. Samson was capable of it, but he didn't discipline himself for it. Luckily for us, our lives aren't yet over, and we can

---

 For more study on how pride is the DNA of every other sin, see Jared C. Wilson's *Seven Daily Sins* (available at *threadsmedia.com*).

 "It is Pride which has been the chief cause of misery in every nation and every family since the world began. Other vices may sometimes bring people together . . . But pride always means enmity." —C.S. Lewis[4]

learn from Samson's mistakes. There's still time to make changes and avoid regrets. Let's spend some time walking through the signs of an undisciplined life.

Sign #1: Compromise

Samson, under his Nazirite vow, was set apart for God. To signify this, he wasn't to touch dead things, eat grapes or drink wine, or cut his hair. We've learned that Samson didn't keep that covenant. He was down in a vineyard and up to no good. He touched not only a dead lion, but in our study in this session, he took up the fresh jawbone of a donkey. He was doing the Lord's work so he thought it was OK, but he was wrong.

Partial obedience to God is always complete disobedience.

> **"But be doers of the word and not hearers only, deceiving yourselves. Because if anyone is a hearer of the word and not a doer, he is like a man looking at his own face in a mirror. For he looks at himself, goes away, and immediately forgets what kind of man he was. But the one who looks intently into the perfect law of freedom and perseveres in it, and is not a forgetful hearer but one who does good works—this person will be blessed in what he does" (James 1:22-25).**

When have you compromised your beliefs for temporary gratification? What was the result?

What distinguishes a "doer" of the word from a "hearer"?

Sign #2: Prayerlessness

Scripture records two specific times Samson prayed, and in both instances, God answered. Samson asked God to give him water, and God did (Judges 15:18). Later, as we'll discover at the end of Samson's life, he asked God to give him strength one last time, and God answered (Judges 16:28). In both instances, Samson's motivation was still self-centered.

Samson failed to tap into the full power of prayer, even though his prayers were effective. The examples we read indicate that Samson's typical prayer happened when he was in a bind. His prayers were all about getting his will done, not accomplishing God's will. It seems Samson didn't use prayer as a means to remain in conversation with God.

 In the New Testament, *obedience* means "to hear or to listen in a state of submission" or "to trust."

Prayer is the ultimate way we communicate with God. It's how we take our frustrations, concerns, joys, sorrows, and thankfulness and lay them at the feet of the Father. Prayer is one way we grow closer to and more like Christ. It's an essential act for those seeking God's purpose for their lives.

> **"Therefore let us approach the throne of grace with boldness, so that we may receive mercy and find grace to help us at the proper time" (Hebrews 4:16).**

Do you have a tendency to call on God only when faced with difficulty? What should be our approach to prayer?

What does your prayer routine look like? What are the benefits of making prayer a routine? Are there any drawbacks?

And when you don't know how to pray, when you're out of words or just aren't sure what to ask for, remember Romans 8:26-27:

> **"In the same way the Spirit also joins to help in our weakness, because we do not know what to pray for as we should, but the Spirit Himself intercedes for us with unspoken groanings. And He who searches the hearts knows the Spirit's mind-set, because He intercedes for the saints according to the will of God."**

Sign #3: Selfishness

Time and again we've seen examples of Samson's self-focus. He fixated on pleasing himself and avenging those who had wronged him without stopping to consider God's role in each situation. He allowed pride, anger, ambition, lust, and plain curiosity to rule his life. However, Jesus said, the goal of our lives boils down to one command to focus solely on God:

> **"Love the Lord your God with all your heart, with all your soul, with all your mind, and with all your strength" (Mark 12:30).**

 We all connect to God in unique ways. Try taking Monvee's spiritual assessment to see how you best connect with God (*monvee.com*).

Jesus boils down the essence of the Christian life to one commandment: love God with everything you have. When you love God first, your other obligations and priorities fall into place. Loving God is the litmus test against which you are to judge your motivations, actions, and commitments. Loving God supremely is the most important commandment, and as Christians, you give Him priority over everything else. You don't love God to the exclusion of loving others. Loving God is what enables you to love others.

What person, attitude, or situation keeps you from focusing on God?

In Mark 12:30, Jesus was referring to our affections, spirit, intelligence, and our will. Considering past choices, which of these cause you to be the most egotistical? Why?

What are some practical signs of a lack of discipline in your life? Do any of the above signs resonate with you?

If we desire to be maximized for God's glory rather than waste our lives, we must do one simple thing: We must pursue a daily walk with Christ.

CULTIVATING YOUR SPIRITUAL LIFE
To be a man or woman of God requires discipline. It requires spiritual exercise and diligence. Samson was a man of physical strength who underachieved. On the other hand, the apostle Paul is an example of a man of physical weakness who overachieved when it came to serving God. The difference, I believe, was daily devotion to God and discipline for God's purpose.

> "But have nothing to do with irreverent and silly myths. Rather, train yourself in godliness, for the training of the body has a limited benefit, but godliness is beneficial in every way, since it holds promise for the present life and also for the life to come" (1 Timothy 4:7-8).

 In Mark 12:30, Jesus was referencing the *Shema* in Deuteronomy 6:4-5, containing the essence of God's covenant with Israel. He expressed the importance of first ingraining His words into our hearts, and then putting them into action.

There are many ways to cultivate your spiritual life. Let's walk through four of them.

1. Read the Bible daily.

If you want to cultivate your spiritual life, you've got to pursue a relationship with God intentionally and purposefully. This isn't just about reforming your behavior or beefing up your religious activity. This is an intentional and intimate experience with God where you seek His presence and His will in your life. The goal is for you to fall more and more in love with God, running to Him for your every need.

Jesus practiced sneaking off to the secret places, away from the crowds to feed His soul and to rest His mind and body. Every day—or at least most days—get alone and spend time with God in His Word, allowing Him time to talk to you and shape your life, strengthen your spirit, and renew your mind through His Word.

If you don't already have one, establish a daily location and time for hearing from God through His Word.

What benefit have you found in daily time in the Word?

How do you feel when you miss that time?

What impact does Bible study have on your spiritual growth?

2. Pray daily.

Talk to God. Ask for help. Tell Him what's on your heart. Believe you have a divine power available and access it.

"Pray constantly" (1 Thessalonians 5:17).

Matthew 7 gives us a peek into the power of prayer:

 Two of the most instructive parables Jesus ever told on prayer (in Luke 11 and Luke 18) encourage not giving up in prayer.

 "The less we read the Word of God, the less we desire to read it, and the less we pray, the less we desire to pray." —George Müller, evangelist[5]

> "Keep asking, and it will be given to you. Keep searching, and you will find. Keep knocking, and the door will be opened to you. For everyone who asks receives, and the one who searches finds, and to the one who knocks, the door will be opened" (vv. 7-8).

It's easy with Samson to shake my head and think, *What an idiot! God answered his prayers. Why didn't he just pray more?* But I wonder if in heaven right now there aren't those watching over us shouting, *Pray, you fool!* I've seen God answer prayers—amazing and impossible prayers.

If you don't currently have a disciplined prayer life, start simple. Take some baby steps and get a loose-leafed notebook. Write down the things and people you're praying for. What do you want God to accomplish in and through you? Then each day—beginning, middle, or end—go through the notebook asking for specific answers. God will answer your prayers. Just give Him the opportunity.

What impossible thing can you trust God for right now?

Do you find prayer life-draining, pointless, or tiring? How can prayer become powerful and life-giving? Ask God to show you.

3. Depend on the Spirit.
Ever seen the TV show (and the movie) *The Beverly Hillbillies*? The theme song will tell you everything you need to know about the show, but basically it's about a poor family who strikes it rich in oil and moves to Beverly Hills, California. The family struck it rich when Jed discovered oil on his land. But the reality is, they could've been millionaires all along; they just lived broke because they hadn't yet tapped into their resources.

In a similar way, we each have a life changer in the Holy Spirit who lives inside us. When we discover God's great gift and allow Him to influence our lives, we will quit living like a spiritual pauper and will begin to live the good life—the God life. We need the Holy Spirit. He's God's gift to us.

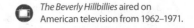

The Beverly Hillbillies aired on American television from 1962–1971.

In Judges 15:14, the Spirit stirred Samson. We're told that the Spirit rushed over him and caused him to prosper and move forward. This is a supernatural empowerment and action of the Spirit of God in the life of a man of God. The same Holy Spirit is available to us every day.

The Holy Spirit affected change in Samson, resulting in obedience. What would you like Him to do in your life?

Do you believe God still works like this today? Explain your response.

When have you seen the Holy Spirit's power most clearly on display in your life? How did you respond to Him?

4. Don't compromise.

Every Christian has three enemies—our flesh, the world in which we live, and the devil. These three try to keep us from living out God's purpose. We must recognize these as our enemies and take them seriously. Don't compromise with them, or you will never overcome them.

> **"As obedient children, do not be conformed to the desires of your former ignorance. But as the One who called you is holy, you also are to be holy in all your conduct; for it is written, Be holy, because I am holy" (1 Peter 1:14-16).**

None of us are sinless or perfect, but that doesn't mean we should tolerate sin in our hearts or lives. Note the word "former" in the passage above. God has changed us, and we're called to move forward. Strive daily to live a life given wholly to God. God has called us to flee from sin and flee toward Himself.

What changes need to be made to allow you to make uncompromised decisions?

 Leading a group? Find extra questions and teaching tools in the leader kit, available for purchase at *threadsmedia.com/samson*.

How are you being obedient to God's call today?

If you knew you couldn't fail, what would you do right now? (Don't forget, you have the Holy Spirit in you and the God of creation behind you!)

APPLY TO LIFE

> **PRAYER:** *Holy Spirit, rise up in me and fill my mind. Take over my life and my days. Let me think Your thoughts. Let me speak Your words with my mouth. Empower the work of my hands today. Guide my feet to where You want me to be. Influence my mind with Your thoughts and the Word of God. Give me all that You are. I want every fruit that You bring and every gift that You want to give me. I declare that You are a Spirit within me of love, of power, and of discipline to do the things through Your strength that I could not do on my own. Fill me up. I confess and renounce all sin that would short-circuit Your power in my life. Have Your way and glorify Your name in and through me right now, amen.*

> **OBSERVE:** This week, take note of how you spend your time. Keep a log of every minute of your day. Document your life in 30-minute blocks. This is a tedious exercise, but it will reveal how you spend your time and how much free time you could have in a day. Next week, review the log before your week starts. Make changes to intentionally block out time for God.

> **LISTEN:** Purchase "Hope for Us All" by Je'kob (feat. The December Keys), "One Thing Remains" by Passion (feat. Kristian Stanfill), and "Wake Up" by All Sons & Daughters (see the playlist at *threadsmedia.com/samson*). Add these to your regular mix of music throughout the week so that you'll be reminded to continue to pursue a daily relationship with Christ.

PURITY RENEWED

Don't control your sex drive.

5

If you were familiar at all with Samson prior to this study, it's likely because you've heard of his sexual exploits, namely with Delilah. Not much has changed since the days of Samson. Our culture has managed to continually turn something wonderful into something cheap, easy, casual, and common. Giving in to sexual desires certainly wasn't God's purpose for Samson's life—and it's not His intention for physical intimacy today. Sex is God's gift to us. It's a good thing, a blessing from God. But we can't misuse the gift without getting burned.

God's desire for us is clear. First Thessalonians 4 lays out His plan:

> **"For this is God's will, your sanctification: that you abstain from sexual immorality, so that each of you knows how to control his own body in sanctification and honor, not with lustful desires, like the Gentiles who don't know God. This means one must not transgress against and defraud his brother in this matter, because the Lord is an avenger of all these offenses, as we also previously told and warned you. For God has not called us to impurity but to sanctification. Therefore, the person who rejects this does not reject man, but God, who also gives you His Holy Spirit" (vv. 3-8).**

How would you summarize God's plan for sex, based on these verses?

What part of His plan do you find most difficult to follow?

Sex, at its core, is about honoring God. In *Birds and Bees,* author Gregg Matte spends time walking through 1 Thessalonians in great detail. But here's his summary of God's plan:

> "To put it simply, then, sex is about pleasing God. And a mature view of sex begins with a desire to follow Him—not just to follow the rules or avoid consequences. . . . According to God's plan, sex is honorable. Sex is to be highly valued. It isn't casual, dirty, unnatural, embarrassing, shameful, scarring, or scary. It's a wonderful part of His creation to bring pleasure and to further creation within the marriage bed. God has lifted sex up to a high and holy level—not to prevent us from attaining the standard, but to make sure we truly respect and appreciate it."[1]

 Watch the *Samson* video for Session 5,
available at *threadsmedia.com/samson.*

SESSION FIVE SAMSON

How is this view different from what you were taught as a kid—indirectly or directly?

What blessings can you identify from faithfully following (or returning to) God's plan?

God understands how hard this fight for purity can be—learning how to control desires and keeping sex in its holy and honorable place. The battle isn't easy, as the Bible paints a clear picture that lust wars against our soul:

> **"Dear friends, I urge you as strangers and temporary residents to abstain from fleshly desires that war against you" (1 Peter 2:11).**

Samson's life teaches us the importance of staying determined in the daily decision to remain pure, set apart for God's purposes. For all his strength, Samson was weak. No enemy could overthrow him. But in the end, because of his selfishness, his inability to follow God's plan for his life, and ultimately, as we'll see in this session, because of his unwillingness to control his sexual urges, Samson imploded.

Staying sexually pure isn't easy. In Samson's case, he allowed his earthly desires to overtake his desire to follow God. But it doesn't have to be that way for us. Regardless of what decisions you've made so far, the future hasn't yet been determined.

Let's look once again at Samson's story and see how his decisions further removed him from God's plan. Then we'll evaluate where we are in the process and come up with a game plan for winning the battle for purity.

Looking back over Sessions 1-5, what part of Samson's story has connected with you most so far? Explain.

THE SLOW SLIDE OF SEXUAL TEMPTATION
In the first session, we discussed how Samson's father Manoah's lack of leadership affected Samson's decisions. Yet every person has a point in which they can no longer allow their upbringing to affect the choices they make. In that session we learned that one of Samson's

It doesn't take a follower of Jesus to understand the lure of sexual temptation. Oscar Wilde once wrote, "I can resist everything except temptation."[2]

greatest flaws was his inability or unwillingness to control his sexual appetite. We'll begin there and walk through each of Samson's strikes against a life of purity.

Strike 1: Compromised Choices

Samson's struggle with sexual temptation started early, and he battled it his whole life. It's one of the first things we read about him. Let's go back to Judges 14 and review the first compromised choice we find in the Samson story:

> **"Samson went down to Timnah and saw a young Philistine woman there. He went back and told his father and his mother: 'I have seen a young Philistine woman in Timnah. Now get her for me as a wife.' But his father and mother said to him, 'Can't you find a young woman among your relatives or among any of our people? Must you go to the uncircumcised Philistines for a wife?' But Samson told his father, 'Get her for me, because I want her'" (vv. 1-3).**

We aren't told anything about Samson's youth. Scriptural documentation of Samson's life jumps from his birth to his infatuation with a beautiful Philistine woman. Old Testament law forbade intermarrying with a person who was not a Jew (Deuteronomy 7:3-4; this command is repeated in the New Testament in 2 Corinthians 6:14-18), but Samson loved what he saw. She was clearly the wrong girl, but he wanted to marry her anyway. Sex was the basis of his relationship, and physical attraction was the primary factor.

As we'll learn, none of Samson's women were called "wise," "spiritually strong," or "virtuous." His sole criteria could be summed up in a single phrase: "Get her for me, for she looks good to me" (Judges 14:3, NASB). Unfortunately, his runaway libido wouldn't let him see the trouble that was coming.

Why was it wrong for Samson to want to marry the Philistine woman?

What other compromised choices did Samson make?

What compromised choices have you made or been tempted to make?

....

 Every major crisis in Samson's life resulting in clashes against the Philistines was brought on by his relationships with Philistine women.

If you're single, what qualities do you look for in a future spouse? If you're married, what qualities do you love about your spouse?

Strike 2: Losing All Sense of Purity

Gaza was one of the five major cities of the Philistines, a distinct stronghold, which is significant because Samson's voyage there brought to light a major flaw: He constantly and carelessly revealed his weaknesses to his enemies.

> "Samson went to Gaza, where he saw a prostitute and went to bed with her. When the Gazites heard that Samson was there, they surrounded the place and waited in ambush for him all that night at the city gate. While they were waiting quietly, they said, 'Let us wait until dawn; then we will kill him.' But Samson stayed in bed until midnight when he got up, took hold of the doors of the city gate along with the two gateposts, and pulled them out, bar and all. He put them on his shoulders and took them to the top of the mountain overlooking Hebron" (Judges 16:1-3).

How do you respond to this passage?

What other flaws about Samson are revealed in this passage?

Samson wasn't spiritually on guard, which left him vulnerable to both his enemies and temptation. He didn't necessarily go to Gaza to see this prostitute, but once he was there and saw her, sparks began to fly in his sex drive. His carelessness led him to forfeit his purity. It seems that for Samson, sex was pretty casual.

The march with the gates covered 38 miles—just one way Samson flexed his muscles. His display struck fear into the hearts of the Philistines and revealed how invincible he thought his brute force made him. Samson had power without purity, and strength without self-control.

Proverbs promises, "Pride comes before destruction, and an arrogant spirit before a fall" (Proverbs 16:18). Its promise doesn't let us down. Samson's self-delusion led him to

 Pride is rebellion against God, because it attributes to one's own self the honor and glory due to God alone. Some consider pride to be the root and essence of all sin.

think that his actions would receive no consequences. He misunderstood God's grace. The more he sinned, it seemed the more of God's grace he experienced. But don't be fooled as Samson was:

> "Should we continue in sin so that grace may multiply? Absolutely not! How can we who died to sin still live in it? . . . Now if we died with Christ, we believe that we will also live with Him, because we know that Christ, having been raised from the dead, will not die again. Death no longer rules over Him. For in light of the fact that He died, He died to sin once for all; but in light of the fact that He lives, He lives to God. So, you too consider yourselves dead to sin but alive to God in Christ Jesus. Therefore do not let sin reign in your mortal body, so that you obey its desires. And do not offer any parts of it to sin as weapons for unrighteousness. But as those who are alive from the dead, offer yourselves to God, and all the parts of yourselves to God as weapons for righteousness. For sin will not rule over you, because you are not under law but under grace" (Romans 6:1-2,8-14).

What motivates you to fight for purity? What motivates you to die to sin?

If we're dead to sin, how is it that we still sin? What does it mean to become "weapons for righteousness"?

How does the knowledge of your death to sin affect your struggle with sin, or how can it affect it moving forward?

Strike 3: Becoming Enslaved

What Samson sowed in Gaza he reaped in Sorek with Delilah. His life choices were about to catch up to him. As the story continued, Samson met a woman named Delilah and fell in love.

> "Some time later, he fell in love with a woman named Delilah, who lived in the Sorek Valley" (Judges 16:4).

 One of the original bad girls of the Bible, Delilah's femme fatale personality is still referenced in modern-day songs, operas, TV shows, books, and movies.

Up to this point, it seems Samson had never been in love before; he had only been in "lust." This time, though, it included his heart. Unfortunately, three problems with Delilah are evident from this one verse:

1) Delilah was from the valley of Sorek. Sorek, according to *The Expositors Bible Commentary,* means "choice vine." Perhaps this is a hint that Samson's Nazirite vow was in grave danger.

2) Delilah's name itself literally means "to bring low" or "to hang." Some say she was a devotee, or a temple prostitute. Either way she was bad news, not the kind of girl you take home to meet your momma.

3) Delilah was not a godly woman: She came from the very people who were enemies of the Israelites, who Samson had been called to protect.

Samson and Delilah weren't married, as far as we know, but we do know Samson had settled into an immoral lifestyle. In this game, three strikes happen quickly. Before you know it, your purity is slipping away.

Have you ever found yourself sliding down this slippery slope? What stopped your slide? What steps have you taken to make sure you never make that first strike again?

The Philistines learned a lesson the last time they tried to trap Samson. This time they wooed his girl with wealth. Samson should have remembered what happened the last time he told a girl a secret: She blabbed it to the wrong people. History has a way of repeating itself.

"The Philistine leaders went to her and said, 'Persuade him to tell you where his great strength comes from, so we can overpower him, tie him up, and make him helpless. Each of us will then give you 1,100 pieces of silver.' So Delilah said to Samson, 'Please tell me, where does your great strength come from? How could someone tie you up and make you helpless?' Samson told her, 'If they tie me up with seven fresh bowstrings that have not been dried, I will become weak and be like any other man.' The Philistine leaders brought her seven fresh bowstrings that had not been dried, and she tied him up with them. While the men in ambush were waiting in her room, she called out to him, 'Samson, the Philistines are here!' But he snapped the bowstrings as a strand of yarn snaps when it touches fire. The secret of his strength remained

 "Samson when strong and brave strangled a lion, but he could not strangle his own loves. He burst the fetters of his foes, but not the cords of his own lusts." —Ambrose, Christian theologian[3]

unknown. Then Delilah said to Samson, 'You have mocked me and told me lies! Won't you please tell me how you can be tied up?' He told her, 'If they tie me up with new ropes that have never been used, I will become weak and be like any other man.' Delilah took new ropes, tied him up with them, and shouted, 'Samson, the Philistines are here!' But while the men in ambush were waiting in her room, he snapped the ropes off his arms like a thread" (Judges 16:5-12).

The lords of the Philistines offered Delilah 1,100 pieces of silver from each of them if she could identify the source of Samson's strength. And it was a challenge she accepted. In this passage, the word "entice" means "to open, make wide, to be simple." The word gives us the idea of seduction, for which Samson is a sucker. It was his Achilles' heel and it ultimately led to his death.

Delilah all but told Samson she was trying to kill him, and he failed to see what she was doing, allowing his pride and sexual desires to blind him to the danger ahead. Perhaps Samson was confident he would never tell her the truth. He just knew he was stronger than she was, so he continued to play with fire.

By the time we get to the next verses, Delilah was no longer playing it cool. Instead, she kicked things into high gear, and Samson came dangerously close to telling her his secret.

"Then Delilah said to Samson, 'You have mocked me all along and told me lies! Tell me how you can be tied up.' He told her, 'If you weave the seven braids on my head with the web of a loom—' She fastened the braids with a pin and called to him, 'Samson, the Philistines are here!' He awoke from his sleep and pulled out the pin, with the loom and the web. 'How can you say, "I love you,"' she told him, 'when your heart is not with me? This is the third time you have mocked me and not told me what makes your strength so great!'" (vv. 13-15).

Delilah urged him for the full truth. There was one urge he understood most and best, and she finally pressed his button. It's certainly possible he was beyond annoyed so he caved, but it's just as likely he was addicted to love. More accurately, Samson was addicted to lust, so he told her everything she asked.

"Because she nagged him day after day and pleaded with him until she wore him out, he told her the whole truth and said to her, 'My hair has never been cut, because I am a Nazirite to God from birth. If I am shaved, my strength will leave me, and I will become weak and be like any other man'" (Judges 16:16-17).

 The word "nagged" is only attributed specifically to two women in Scripture, and both were Samson's mistresses.

Why might Samson have finally given in to Delilah?

What drains your spiritual strength?

Samson knew the call of God on his life, and the source of his strength. Yet he was so enslaved that he didn't even realize when the last of his Nazirite vow had been broken, causing the Lord to depart from him:

> "When Delilah realized that he had told her the whole truth, she sent this message to the Philistine leaders: 'Come one more time, for he has told me the whole truth.' The Philistine leaders came to her and brought the money with them. Then she let him fall asleep on her lap and called a man to shave off the seven braids on his head. In this way, she made him helpless, and his strength left him. Then she cried, 'Samson, the Philistines are here!' When he awoke from his sleep, he said, 'I will escape as I did before and shake myself free.' But he did not know that the LORD had left him. The Philistines seized him and gouged out his eyes. They brought him down to Gaza and bound him with bronze shackles, and he was forced to grind grain in the prison. But his hair began to grow back after it had been shaved" (Judges 16:18-22).

Samson's pride allowed his self-indulgence to consume him, and it led to his capture by the Philistines. The hand of God that made Samson great left him, and he, clearly nothing without God, became a slave. Samson was no longer in control of his own life, but others would control his fate. He was chained and blinded. A man with great strength from the hand of God had planned to be free, but the bonds of sin aren't so easily shaken off.

Have you ever lost something you loved because of sin? Was it a sin you committed? Or someone else's sin?

If it was your own sin, do you still feel guilt and shame because of it?

 Listen to "Your Love Is Louder" by An Epic, No Less and "Restore" by Chris August from the *Samson* playlist, available at *threadsmedia.com/samson*.

What have you done to try to move on and pursue God's best?

It doesn't matter who you are, how strong, how famous, how wealthy, or how pretty; in the end, sin kills. You lose control of your life when you become enslaved to sin. The judge can take away your kids, your spouse can take away your money and your marriage, and your boss can take away your job. All we have to lean on is our relationship with and devotion to God.

A LITTLE SELF-EVALUATION

I remember the story of a Duke University co-ed who kept a diary of her sexual encounters with Duke athletes. She jokingly called it an experiment, a school project. She made a PowerPoint presentation with pictures and ratings of each guy in several categories. It was intended only for the eyes of her closest friends, but once she e-mailed it and one or two of them shared it with only a couple of trusted friends who did the same, the whole thing went viral. Some of the guys complained that she violated their privacy. Others celebrated her for her sexual freedom.

The problem did not begin with sending the PowerPoint. The problem began when she had casual sex with guys who were little more than total strangers—like she was changing shoes. But sex isn't like changing shoes. It's much more, and when used improperly, it has lasting effects. I like what authors Mark Regnerus and Jeremy Uecker warn about the realities of casual sex in their book *Premarital Sex in America:*

> "Sex is far from a *simple* pleasure. The emotional pain that can linger after poor sexual decision-making, at any age, suggests a complex morality inherent to human sexuality. Some—more men than women—prefer sex without security, which tends to damage others—more women than men—on the inside. Others seem emotionally able to handle relationship instability in their sex lives better than the majority . . . Simplifying and disenchanting human sexuality, however, nets few gains across the population, and is instead more apt to leave unhappiness and fractured relationships in its wake. . . . [M]ost emerging adults will *not* experience an unintended pregnancy or an STI, but have already and will continue to experience regrettable sex."[4]

How have you seen this to be true in your life or in the lives of those around you?

 Leading a group? Find extra questions and teaching tools in the leader kit, available for purchase at *threadsmedia.com/samson.*

This is the current state of our culture. Sex is no big deal. It's "casual" and prevalent in the music we listen to, the billboards we drive by, the movies we watch, and the magazines we purchase (or the ones we glance at in the checkout line). Sex is accessible, too. You can find it online in complete anonymity. Some cities even brag about their offering: "what happens here stays here." It's easy to compare ourselves to others or justify those things we're comfortable with doing. Regardless of what the culture says, regret was never intended to be a standard feeling when it comes to sex. We're called to follow God's lead and to honor Him in every area of our lives. That certainly includes our purity.

It's time to evaluate your own heart and take stock of where you are in your battle, or lack thereof, against sexual sin.

Are you battling strong?
Sexual temptation is a fight for everybody. I bought my 8-year-old son a pack of wrestling trading cards. One day after we went through the car wash, I emptied my trash out of my truck and was about to pull away. My son said, "Dad, stop the truck." I asked, "Why?" "I've got to throw this one away," he said. It was a picture of a half-clad diva.

Sexual temptation starts so much earlier than we expect. We have to be prepared to battle strong against temptation at any age, whether single or married. Self-control isn't easy. The battle is tough. But it's more important than you could ever imagine.

> **"Don't you know that the runners in a stadium all race, but only one receives the prize? Run in such a way to win the prize. Now everyone who competes exercises self-control in everything. However, they do it to receive a crown that will fade away, but we a crown that will never fade away. Therefore I do not run like one who runs aimlessly or box like one beating the air. Instead, I discipline my body and bring it under strict control, so that after preaching to others, I myself will not be disqualified" (1 Corinthians 9:24-27).**

What things have you attributed this passage to in the past? How do these verses encourage you to battle strong for purity?

Are you vulnerable?
If you're vulnerable, you have the desire to be strong, but temptation is knocking at your door and you're thinking about answering it. You haven't completely given in yet, but you are in full compromise mode. Time and again, Samson thought he could handle temptation but he failed.

 According to an ABC News poll, 29 percent of people have sex on their first date, and 30 percent of men age 30 and older have paid for sex.[5]

Don't compromise with the books you read, the shows you watch, the places you frequent, or the people you hang out with. Once you start down that slope, it grows increasingly slippery. Don't mess with temptation. Temptation always looks good. It looks fun and fulfilling and promises freedom, but in the end it will take you down. Resist the Devil!

> "Therefore, submit to God. But resist the Devil, and he will flee from you. Draw near to God, and He will draw near to you. Cleanse your hands, sinners, and purify your hearts, double-minded people! Be miserable and mourn and weep. Your laughter must change to mourning and your joy to sorrow. Humble yourselves before the Lord, and He will exalt you" (James 4:7-10).

When it comes to "an innocent look," where is the line between "temptation" and "sin"?

What are some practical things you can do to "submit to God"? To "resist the Devil"?

What people or places tempt you to compromise your beliefs? What can you do to reduce or eliminate the lure?

Have you been giving in?
You know what's in front of you is wrong, but you're doing it anyway. Maybe you're trying to justify it in your mind. But if you have to justify what you're doing, it likely means you're doing the wrong thing. Through Christ, you've been made alive. You don't have to go on sinning. You have the power within you to change the way things have been, to be more intentional with your relationships.

If you've given in recently, can you identify why? How does it make you feel? What can you commit to change?

Do you feel enslaved?
If you're enslaved, you can't stop going, looking, and indulging. You feel trapped, with no good way out. Maybe you want to stop, but you keep feeling pulled in. Perhaps you're addicted to the emotional or physical high, yet literally dying from moving further and

 For further study on God's plan for sex, check out *Birds and Bees: A conversation about God, sex, and sexuality* by Gregg Matte (available at *threadsmedia.com*).

further away from your relationship with God. On the matter of desire and temptation, Dietrich Bonhoeffer wrote,

> "With irresistible power desire seizes mastery over the flesh. All at once a secret, smouldering fire is kindled. The flesh burns and is in flames. It makes no difference whether it is sexual desire, or ambition, or vanity, or desire for revenge, or love of fame and power, or greed of money, or finally, that strange desire for the beauty of the world, of nature. Joy in God is in course of being extinguished in us and we seek all our joy in the creature. At this moment God is quite unreal to us, he loses all reality, and only desire for the creature is real; the only reality is the devil. Satan does not here fill us with hatred of God, but with forgetfulness of God. And now his falsehood is added to this proof of strength. The lust thus aroused envelops the mind and will of man in deepest desires. The powers of clear discrimination and of decision are taken from us."[6]

That is a picture of a person enslaved.

Why do you think that we humans have such a pull toward something we know we can't/aren't supposed to touch?

Which of the titles fits you best right now—battling strong, vulnerable, giving in, or enslaved?

HOW TO OVERCOME TEMPTATION
Now that we've identified some points of weakness, let's talk about how to become successful in the fight against temptation.

1. Get Honest.
If you continue on this secretive path, things are not going to end well for you. Solomon, on seduction, said, "He follows her impulsively like an ox going to the slaughter, like a deer bounding toward a trap until an arrow pierces its liver, like a bird darting into a snare—he doesn't know it will cost him his life" (Proverbs 7:22-23). Recognize where you are, what kinds of decisions you've been making, and be honest with yourself. No matter how strong you may think you are, temptation can easily pull you in and take you down a road you never intended to drive on.

 If you're a man struggling with sexual issues, consider finding a Samson society group in your area. Learn more at *samsonsociety.com*.

What lies, excuses, or justifications have you made regarding lust and sex? Confess those now to yourself and to God.

2. Get Serious.

Immorality is indicative of the flesh, not life in the spirit (1 Corinthians 6:9-10; 15-20). It's time to get serious about this. Life and death and eternity hang in the balance. It's not worth fiddling with, acting like it's not a problem, and doing nothing about it. Get serious about battling your issue—as simple or as complex as that struggle may be. Pursue God with everything that you have.

Would you say your view of sex is casual or treasured, guilt-ridden, or worthy of God's blessing?

3. Get Away.

If you're going to walk with God, there may be drastic changes that need to be made in your life. Those changes may involve your friends, your job, your neighborhood, the places you shop, the books you read, the movies you watch, or even your entire lifestyle. But God says no price is too high to pay for your purity and godly character (Matthew 5:27-30).

What changes need to be made in your life to better follow God's plan? How can Samson's story encourage you to stay focused on those changes?

4. Get a Positive Pursuit.

Second Timothy 2:22 encourages us to "flee," but it also shows us the other side of the coin: a positive pursuit. In place of the negative, we've got to pursue something good (see Ephesians 4:22-32).

What are some good things you could pursue in place of a sin?

5. Get into the Word.

David, the psalmist, knew about the power of temptation. He wrote,

> **"How can a young man keep his way pure? By keeping Your word. I have sought You with all my heart; don't let me wander from Your commands. I have treasured Your word in my heart so that I may not sin against You"** (Psalm 119:9-11).

 Not sure what it looks like to "get away"? Joseph gives us a pretty good example in Genesis 39:6-12.

When has God's Word helped you overcome a difficult situation in the past?

Jesus, when tempted, quoted Scripture (Matthew 4:1-10). If temptation is a lie and an illusion, Scripture is the truth and the hammer that breaks the smoke and mirrors. The Bible doesn't guarantee your purity. Neither does following Jesus. But the Scriptures give you power to fight (1 Corinthians 10:13).

We read in Judges 16:22 that Samson's hair began to grow back. What was the result of sinful choices and actions that dishonored God (a shaved head) was now the fertile ground of God's grace.

Some of us understand moral failure all too well. Scars and scabs mark our lives. We've fallen into temptation and we carry great shame. As Christians, we aren't perfect; we're just forgiven. Our metaphorical hair will grow again and God will use us. Let His mercy reign over you today.

APPLY TO LIFE

> PRAY: Ask God to give you the courage this week to step up and do something about your purity. It's never too late to pursue purity, and you can honor God by choosing it now. Pray that you would take the necessary steps starting this week.

> OBSERVE: What are the habits you have in your life that, in order to feel good about them, you have to justify? Maybe you have to justify them to God, to yourself, or to others. This week, notice the times you justify your behavior.

> STUDY: Go back over Ephesians 4:22-32, looking at the "put off/put on" principle. What really happens if you "put off" but don't "put on." According to verse 32, how do you think putting on these characteristics imitates Christ?

> LISTEN: Purchase "Your Love Is Louder" by An Epic, No Less and "Restore" by Chris August (see the playlist at *threadsmedia.com/samson*). Add these to your regular mix of music throughout the week to focus on God-honoring decisions.

CALLING
REPURPOSED

Give up hope.

Life can sometimes resemble sports in that for some, every new year brings a renewed sense of hope and optimism. For others, it brings renewed frustrations over coaches, players, and traditions. But when it comes to the contrast between sports and life, there's one glaring difference—life actually does matter. But who among us hasn't blown it? Who among us hasn't failed to live up to expectations, crashing and burning in a big way? Who among us hasn't needed a "next year" or wished the whole thing would just go away? Shame can quickly sink us into despair, and we face a crossroads: Hunker down and live in last year's failures and hopelessness, or turn the page and start a new chapter with a new hope. The sports team that turns the page does better the next year. And so will you.

We've come to the end of the story of a hero who needed new hope. Samson was born with incredible potential and expectations. But strings of bad decisions, putting himself in the wrong situations, surrounding himself with the wrong people, and choosing to dishonor God left Samson powerless. This once-strong hero was reduced to humiliating labor. As we'll see, though, God worked through even a disobedient son like Samson to protect His people and glorify His name. The question is, how much more could He have done if Samson had chosen to faithfully serve Him? My prayer throughout this session is that Samson's story would help you learn how to rediscover hope and engage your God-given purpose.

SAMSON'S LAST DECISION

In Session 5, we left Samson blind, bound, and grinding grain. Now we find him summoned to a festival. The party is on in Gaza. These verses give us a picture of what sin will do.

> "Now the Philistine leaders gathered together to offer a great sacrifice to their god Dagon. They rejoiced and said: Our god has handed over our enemy Samson to us. When the people saw him, they praised their god and said: Our god has handed over to us our enemy who destroyed our land and who multiplied our dead. When they were drunk, they said, 'Bring Samson here to entertain us.' So they brought Samson from prison, and he entertained them. They had him stand between the pillars. Samson said to the young man who was leading him by the hand, 'Lead me where I can feel the pillars supporting the temple, so I can lean against them.' The temple was full of men and women; all the leaders of the Philistines were there, and about 3,000 men and women were on the roof watching Samson entertain them" (Judges 16:23-27).

 Watch the *Samson* video for Session 6, available at *threadsmedia.com/samson*.

Who or what was responsible for Samson's demise?

What explanation is there for the Philistines not killing Samson?

Sin makes a mockery of God.

The Philistines didn't plan to kill Samson immediately, giving them the opportunity to have a celebration of their god. Samson gave the enemy of God an opportunity to blaspheme. In their understanding, their god, Dagon, had defeated Samson's God Yahweh (Judges 16:23). Let the truth be known, though: Samson fell into their hands not because Dagon had defeated the Lord, but because Samson's sinfulness had caused the God of Israel to abandon him. God was being mocked, and Samson was painfully aware that it was his fault. This is great motivation to faithfulness for us, to give our all as followers of Jesus to avoid disappointing or defaming God.

Do you ever feel like your actions have reflected badly on Christianity? What happened?

What was your response to your own failure and its implications?

Sin made a joke out of Samson.

Samson was supposed to wipe out the enemy and make them run. Instead, he served as half-time entertainment for their party. Judges 16:25 tells us that all the lords of the Philistines gathered together in an atmosphere similar to the Super Bowl. They were drunk and decided to bring Samson out for some fun and games. He served as their amusement. They laughed, mocked, hated, and made sport of him. As the winning "team," they wanted to mess with him and take joy in their victory.

Like the cover of a tabloid tell-all, in this moment Samson's past laid exposed on the arena floor revealing every gross detail. Samson had lusted with his eyes, and now his eyes were gone. He had no self-control, but now there was no need—he had been bound by chains. He chased after women, and now he was doing a woman's work. He played games in Gaza and toyed with temptation; now he was the game and they were toying with him.

 Faithful can be defined as steadfast, dedicated, dependable, and worthy of trust. Faithful God keeps His covenant, and faithful people keep His commandments.

Samson suffered devastating consequences of his sin.

What emotions do you think Samson felt in this moment?

What do you consider to be the most tragic part of Samson's life so far?

SAMSON'S RESTORED PURPOSE

Here we come to the end of Samson's story. Blind, shackled, and mocked, Samson called out to God for the last time.

> **"He called out to the LORD: 'Lord GOD, please remember me. Strengthen me, God, just once more. With one act of vengeance, let me pay back the Philistines for my two eyes.' Samson took hold of the two middle pillars supporting the temple and leaned against them, one on his right hand and the other on his left. Samson said, 'Let me die with the Philistines.' He pushed with all his might, and the temple fell on the leaders and all the people in it. And the dead he killed at his death were more than those he had killed in his life. Then his brothers and his father's family came down, carried him back, and buried him between Zorah and Eshtaol in the tomb of his father Manoah. So he judged Israel 20 years" (Judges 16:28-31).**

Samson was weak, he was blind, and he was mocked. Yet he trusted God and God gave him strength. God used Samson's life to glorify His great name—despite his lust-driven decisions, his broken Nazirite vow, and the wake of destruction he left at every turn.

God is in the business of restoring those who trust Him. Forgiveness is not just a nice word; it's a blessed reality for anyone who claims the promise of 1 John 1:

> **"If we say, 'We have no sin,' we are deceiving ourselves, and the truth is not in us. If we confess our sins, He is faithful and righteous to forgive us our sins and to cleanse us from all unrighteousness" (vv. 8-9).**

How does God's answering Samson's prayer that day support this passage?

....

 Samson called out to God, just as he had in Judges 15:18, asking the Lord to "remember" him. In the Old Testament, to remember meant to act on one's behalf.

God forgives fully. He wipes out our sins. He expunges our past record. He washes us clean. God forgives immediately, not waiting until we clean up our acts or prove our worth. Forgiveness is bought by Jesus and applied the moment we each choose to receive Him, the second we confess to God that we are sorry.

Restoration, though, is gradual.

Samson's hair didn't grow back all at once, but gradually, over time, it did. In the same way, God doesn't restore us to our former positions of responsibility or hand us back our old lives in one fell swoop—partly because He doesn't want us to have our old lives back. He wants us to have new, different lives, ones that are focused on Him and His perfect purposes. Restoration comes as we release our old ways, habits, and deeds, allowing God to slowly rebuild our lives and decision-making ability. As we become new, our purposes are slowly restored.

What might this type of restoration mean for your life?

Although God forgives totally and freely, sometimes sin has sobering consequences. Moses never got into the promised land. David never built the temple. Samson would never again see this side of heaven. Yet Samson regained a measure of his purpose: He wiped out more Philistines at his death than when he was alive. In one act, he fulfilled the beginning of his purpose: "to save Israel from the power of the Philistines" (Judges 13:5). But having not delivered them completely, Samson didn't accomplish the full measure of his purpose. Some consequences are irreversible.

What other consequences from Samson's decisions were irreversible?

Had Samson recognized his sinful tendencies toward pride and lust earlier, do you believe things would have ended differently for him? Explain.

Do you believe that if you can identify your areas of weakness, then your future can be different from your past? What Scriptures give you hope?

 Pride. Lust. Gluttony. Greed. Envy. Sloth. Wrath. We carry these sins around in our hearts daily. To diagnose the root of your sins, read *Seven Daily Sins* by Jared C. Wilson (available at *threadsmedia.com*).

THE HOPE IN SAMSON'S STORY

If you're feeling beaten down because of your sin, now's the time to grasp on to some hope from Samson's story. Let's look at how Samson experienced new, fresh hope.

1. He called to God.

We catch a glimpse of God's grace when Samson's hair began to grow again. It's likely that Samson finally recognized there was one person who had never given up on him, one person who had constantly been there and who had the power to help—so Samson called out to God.

The grace of God is amazing. God had every right to ignore Samson's prayer, but God not only listened to Samson's request, He graciously answered that prayer.

When have you seen God answer an impossible request at a time of great need?

What did His grace mean to you?

2. He humbled himself.

Samson had always been the proud type, but now we see him pleading for God's help. When he found himself in a defenseless situation, he understood his need for God more than ever before.

Samson's prayer, however, contains a lingering hint of selfishness: His request was ultimately about personal revenge. But at the end of the day, Samson was acknowledging that his strength and success came only from the Lord, and if God didn't act, Samson would not be helped.

What would you have to surrender to acknowledge God's strength and power over your life? What step can you take to do that today?

....

 One of the criminals hanging on the cross next to Jesus at His crucifixion asked Him to "remember me" (Luke 23:42). Jesus reassured the man that after death he would immediately be reunited with Him.

3. He reengaged his purpose.

Samson prayed, "God, remember me." I don't think he was asking God to remember his many failures. I believe Samson was praying that God would remember His purpose, plan, and call on Samson's life. In other words, Samson wanted God to accomplish through Samson what he had been set apart to do—despite Samson's inability to do so himself.

Even though it cost Samson his life, he gladly became a martyr.

Which of the above do you feel you need to do today—call to God, humble yourself, or reengage your purpose? Why?

Samson chose to die with the Philistines instead of living enslaved to them, and that's why his death is a tragic end. Could God have used Samson again? Of course! He didn't have eyes, but he had God. Samson didn't have to call it quits. He could have been freed. He could have been given a spirit of wisdom like Solomon. There are more ways to be a great leader for God than just by military might.

Even though he was blind, he still had God.

Think about some people who have impacted our world even though they didn't have their sight: Helen Keller inspired us as an author, activist, and lecturer. Stevie Wonder and Ray Charles have blessed us with great music. Claude Monet, the French impressionist, painted one of his most famous paintings while almost completely blind. Franklin Delano Roosevelt became the 32nd President though his vision was impaired. Harriet Tubman served in the underground railroad that led many slaves to freedom. Louis Braille developed a writing system that allows blind people to read. Marla Runyan became a three-time national champion in the women's 5000 metres, an Olympic athlete, and the top American finisher in the 2002 New York City Marathon though legally blind. Many believe the apostle Paul had eye problems that qualified him as disabled, yet he spread the gospel and dictated letters that became more than half of our New Testament.

Can you relate to Samson's life? Maybe today you're a long way from where you used to be. You used to be a leader in your church, or you used to be married and have a family. You used to be a leader in your youth group. You used to be a virgin. You used to own your own business. You used to be so many things, but not anymore. Now the pieces of your life story lay exposed. Like Samson—shame, anger, regret, and despair darken your life.

 Samson's body was retrieved to be buried with his family, but his period of leadership achieved no rest for the people of Israel.

We all know people who, in moments of bad judgment, made poor decisions that cost themselves and other people dearly.

Satan comes "only to steal and to kill and to destroy" (John 10:10). The ugly side of sin is that the consequences may mean you never get your family, your job, your ministry, or your full purpose back. But if you genuinely repent of your sin and turn to God in faith, God will forgive and begin the restoration process within you. God will use your life again. He delights to use imperfect people for two reasons. First, because that's the only kind He has—we're all imperfect people. Second, He works through imperfect people because He gets all the glory.

Who have you known whose decisions cost them everything?

Has your sin cost you something you dearly loved and cherished? Were the consequences immediate or did they happen over time?

Has God restored your lost treasure? If not, how have you coped with your loss?

Samson's purpose was that he was to be set apart to God and to deliver Israel from the hand of the Philistines. His purpose was wrapped up in the greater purpose of God. God knew the people were sinful so He allowed the enemy to capture them. But God also sent the deliverer to free them. At all times, God was and is in control and working for His purposes.

God wanted Samson's life to be a picture of distinction. Yet Israel was completely compromised and melding in with Philistine culture. Samson was to be a lesson in living color, a living embodiment of separation. He was a man separated from death and wine and razors, but more importantly he was a man separated to God. Unfortunately, Samson never really got it. He only understood what he wasn't supposed to do and only half-heartedly kept that part of the deal.

....

 The Bible explains that a person who constantly and consistently follows a sinful course will become so enmeshed in sin that he or she is enslaved to it (see Romans 6).

YOUR RESTORATIVE PURPOSE

God has a purpose for you. No matter who you are or what you've lost, if you're still on planet Earth, God's purpose for your life isn't done. It's not time to throw in the towel yet. Don't give up! God is in the business of restoration.

God wants to have a relationship with you.

Relationship has been God's desire since the days of Eden. God made humanity for relationship. But our sin destroyed that and marred the heart of our purpose. That's why Jesus came. He came on purpose to restore us to our purpose (see Luke 4:43; 2 Peter 3:9). He wants to walk with us, guiding us toward Him, helping us through all of life's ups and downs.

A vital part of our relationship with God is that it comes through faith. We can't earn salvation with works—a truth that separates Christianity from other major religions. There's only one way to God; He doesn't require diverse paths or rituals in order to have a relationship with Him. Salvation is available to everyone.

> **"God's love was revealed among us in this way: God sent His One and Only Son into the world so that we might live through Him. Love consists in this: not that we loved God, but that He loved us and sent His Son to be the propitiation for our sins" (1 John 4:9-10).**

Why would God want a relationship with us?

What does a relationship with God look like on a daily basis?

God wants you to live for Him and be like Jesus.

When God calls us to holiness (1 Peter 1:14-16), we tend to think of all the things we can't do, missing that we are to be set apart to God. Sadly for Samson, his relationship with God was formal and legalistic, not life-giving.

Maybe you understand spiritual life as just keeping a bunch of rules: things you can't do, places you can't go, dances you can't dance, drinks you can't drink. But abstaining from bad things doesn't mean you are any closer to God. God calls us to a positive, joy-filled

---

 Listen to "Hope Will Lead Us On" by BarlowGirl, "Not the End of Me" by Group 1 Crew, and "Good to Be Alive" by Jason Gray from the *Samson* playlist, available at *threadsmedia.com/samson*.

relationship with Jesus. A truly separated Christian is a believer whose heart and life are set apart to God and who lives life for Him (Ephesians 4:1). God's call on our lives is for life, too. We are to be dedicated to Him in everything for the rest of our lives.

Whoever you are, whatever you've done in the past, forgiveness of sin and the freedom to live for God are available to you as a gift. Through faith in Jesus, a right relationship with God awaits to be credited to your account. Today is a new day, with a fresh start at seeking after God and His desires for you.

> **"Because of the LORD's faithful love we do not perish, for His mercies never end. They are new every morning; great is Your faithfulness! I say: The LORD is my portion, therefore I will put my hope in Him"** (Lamentations 3:22-24).

Although not a Christian theologian, Ralph Waldo Emerson understood the value of living each day to the fullest and not dwelling on the past. He said,

> "Finish every day and be done with it. You have done what you could. Some blunders and some absurdities no doubt crept in; forget them as soon as you can. Tomorrow is a new day; begin it well and serenely with too high a spirit to be encumbered with your old nonsense. This day is all that is good and fair. It is too dear, with its hopes and invitations, to waste a moment on the yesterdays."[1]

What does it mean for you personally that God can use you despite the mistakes you've made?

God wants you to serve His purpose.

Your life is part of a bigger plan. God's purpose for you preceded your birth, just like His purpose for Samson was intact before He ever made Samson.

> **"For we are His creation, created in Christ Jesus for good works, which God prepared ahead of time so that we should walk in them"** (Ephesians 2:10).

We act like knowing our purpose is some big mystery, but in reality it's not so hidden. God didn't keep secret Samson's purpose, but revealed it through a messenger and through his life.

 In the Old Testament, typically God sent an angel or a prophet to reveal His word and purposes for people.

Do you know what your God-given purpose is? If so, how can Samson's story encourage you to persevere in your faith?

IDENTIFYING THE ULTIMATE QUESTION: WHY ARE WE HERE?

If you're unsure of your purpose, stay with me. God can and will use multiple ways to communicate with His people. Let's spend some time looking at just a few ways God may reveal His will for your life.

Through Preaching

Though God can speak through visions and dreams and in miraculous ways, often He speaks through the ordinary avenue of a person: a preacher.

God uses sermons to reveal your purpose. You sit in church and hear about God's promises, His works, His power, and something inside you comes alive. It motivates you to action. That is God speaking. Pay attention to the feelings within you as you worship. It might just be the Holy Spirit guiding you.

Identify one time when the Holy Spirit spoke to you through a worship service. How did that moment change you?

Through Your Past

One of the ways you can discover God's purpose is to look behind you and see where God has been working to shape you. God has given you spiritual gifts (1 Peter 4:10). He's given you a heart and passions, abilities and a personality. God has also given you experiences. Look back on your life, and be reminded that God knows today what tomorrow holds. He will work ahead of you, shaping your life with experiences that uniquely prepare you for your purpose.

You may feel defeated because of your past, but do you know many of the best leaders are those who have overcome great setbacks? Those who have overcome abuse in the past are better equipped to help others overcome abuse. You know who has the most compassion for teenage moms? Those who walked that road before. Guys who excel at helping other men overcome divorce, addiction, and affairs are those who have faced and prevailed over those things themselves. God can redeem your past issues and use them to prepare you for His purpose.

 In Psalm 34:18, we learn that the more we're willing to be real with God, the more likely we are to hear His voice.

"Praise the God and Father of our Lord Jesus Christ, the Father of mercies and the God of all comfort. He comforts us in all our affliction, so that we may be able to comfort those who are in any kind of affliction, through the comfort we ourselves receive from God" (2 Corinthians 1:3-4).

Whether your affliction was brought on by your own choices or that of others, how can God use those experiences to show you His calling for the future?

Through the Scriptures

The primary way we find God's purpose is to look in the Bible. Sin brings captivity and confession brings deliverance. Go with what God is up to. Search the Scriptures to see how God has spoken definitively. He can breathe new life in to our evolving stories today.

"Your word is a lamp for my feet and a light on my path" (Psalm 119:105).

God's Word is the primary way God speaks to us. It is His will revealed. God has spoken to you before. There's no doubt about it. He may even be speaking to you right now as you're reading these words.

How have you heard God speak to you before? What mode did He use?

If you haven't heard God speak to you lately or you want to hear more from Him, develop a plan to spend more time cultivating your relationship with Him. Find a quiet place to pray and read His Word, taking more time to listen than to speak.

LIVING YOUR PURPOSE

Maybe you don't feel like you can really live out God's purpose for you. He's speaking, you're listening, but you just feel weak. If you think you can't do what God is calling you to do, you're actually right—in a way. You can't do it on your own. But God will give you His Spirit and anointing to be able to do whatever He calls you to do, just as He gave Samson the strength when he called upon Him.

 Consider journaling your thoughts as you seek God's will. You'll be greatly encouraged as you can see His hand guiding you, and writing the words will help you flesh out what's running through your head and heart.

God doesn't call the qualified; He qualifies the called. He meets us where we are and gives us the strength to do His work:

> "I am able to do all things through Him who strengthens me" (Philippians 4:13).

How do you respond to this verse, knowing that God will equip you for what's in the future?

Samson lived a self-serving life apart from God's plan, and therefore he didn't achieve the potential deliverance for God's people that could have been possible. But with his last breaths, Samson returned to do what He was made to do. Despite all his failures, Samson is included in the "Hall of Faith," the writer of Hebrew's catalogue of people of God whose faith is worth imitating.

> "And what more can I say? Time is too short for me to tell about Gideon, Barak, Samson, Jephthah, David, Samuel, and the prophets, who by faith conquered kingdoms, administered justice, obtained promises, shut the mouths of lions, quenched the raging of fire, escaped the edge of the sword, gained strength after being weak, became mighty in battle, and put foreign armies to flight" (Hebrews 11:32-34).

Maybe you have had this sense that God called you to serve Him several years ago. You've turned away from it in some way. Maybe you feel like you're lost or you've missed your chance. Let this give you renewed hope: Moses took a detour, spending 40 years in the desert on the back side of nowhere on his way to becoming a great leader. Peter took a little detour, too, denying Jesus and then returning to his old job. Jesus went to him and restored him first spiritually and then as a leader in the Christian church.

One of the most influential books I've ever read, *Ordering Your Private World,* was written by Gordon MacDonald, a successful pastor and author. He served with WorldVision and was president of InterVarsity Christian Fellowship. But MacDonald got off track and compromised his integrity as a husband and minister. In 1987 he admitted to being involved in adultery and stepped away from Christian ministry. He turned away from the affair and back to God and his family. He was restored and returned to ministry. Then he wrote a book, *Rebuilding Your Broken World,* was a speaker at Promise Keeper rallies, and was an advisor to President Clinton during the difficult days of his administration. Though he stumbled, he repented and was restored.

 While we're called to "pray constantly" (1 Thessalonians 5:17), we still need to set aside specific times for prayer. At least once or twice a week, have lunch alone. Find a park or café off the beaten path and spend your lunch hour in private prayer with God.

MacDonald is just one example of countless people who have messed up. Abraham was a liar. Jacob, whose name was changed to Israel, was a con artist who stole his brother's birth-right. Moses killed a man with his bare hands. Rahab welcomed the spies into her home and saved her family. She is one of only five women mentioned in the lineage of Jesus our Savior. But before that, she ran an escort service in the "red light district" of Jericho. David, called a man after God's heart, wrote much of Psalms after his failure and as a result of his being restored by God. Peter became the leader of the church. Noah hit the bottle too hard and acted like a fool before passing out. This wasn't before the ark, nor on the ark. This was after God had been good to him.

What hope do you find in the stories of flawed people whom God used?

Who would you consider successful in their pursuit of God's purpose? Explain.

How can you learn from their examples to not waste what you've been given?

I think God includes stories in Scripture about people like Samson to encourage us to never lose hope. If you've stumbled, there's still hope! God can and will use you again. Confess your mistakes to Him and embrace the newfound hope given to you through His grace:

> **"Where sin multiplied, grace multiplied even more so that, just as sin reigned in death, so also grace will reign through righteousness, resulting in eternal life through Jesus Christ our Lord" (Romans 5:20b-21).**

God's purpose will be done. Will you join your life today to what matters most? Will you set about success at the right things? Your story is not yet finished. God is not through with you; in fact He has great things to do in your life.

Jesus will one day come again. Our purpose until then is to live for God's purpose.

 Leading a group? Find extra questions and teaching tools in the leader kit, available for purchase at *threadsmedia.com/samson*.

APPLY TO LIFE

> **PRAY:** Ask God to reveal or reaffirm His purpose for your life this week. Then be open to His prompting, whether that's through a sermon, the Scriptures, or through looking back over your past.

> **STUDY:** Search the Scriptures. Find the times in the Bible when God called men and women to specific tasks and purposes. Write those down, and evaluate what God may be calling you to.

> **LISTEN:** Purchase "Hope Will Lead Us On" by BarlowGirl, "Not the End of Me" by Group 1 Crew, and "Good to Be Alive" by Jason Gray (see the playlist at *threadsmedia.com/ samson*). Add these to your regular mix of music throughout the week to remember the hope found in God's purposes for you.

END NOTES

SESSION 1

1. Adapted from W. Wayne Vanhorn, "The Judges in Judges," *Biblical Illustrator* Magazine (Nashville: LifeWay Christian Resources of the Southern Baptist Convention, Summer 2012), 6-9.
2. Victor Parachin, "The Fine Art of Good Fathering," *Herald of Holiness* Magazine (Kansas City, MO: Nazarene Publishing House, February 1995), 32-33.
3. Terry Ann-Craigie, "Effects of Paternal Presence and Family Instability on Child Cognitive Performance, Center for Research on Child Wellbeing Working Paper 2008-03-FF," (Michigan State University Department of Economics: November 17, 2008), 7. Available from the Internet: *crcw.princeton.edu/workingpapers/WP08-03-FF.pdf*.
4. Sarah Allen, Ph.D., and Kerry Daly, Ph.D., "The Effects of Father Involvement: An Updated Research Summary of the Evidence Inventory" (University of Guelph: Centre for Families, Work & Well-Being, 2007).
5. Donnie L. Martin, "Favored by Faithful Fathers," a sermon on Proverbs 17:6. Available from the Internet: *www.pastorlife.com*.
6. Richard Innes, "Healing a Man's Father Wound." Available from the Internet: *www.actsweb.org*.
7. Mike Genung, "Healing Father Wounds," excerpted from the *The Road to Grace: Finding True Freedom from the Bondage of Sexual Addiction* (Colorado Springs: Blazing Grace, 2005). Available from the Internet: *www.urbanministry.org*.
8. Horn, W., & Sylvester, T. (2002). (p. 95); Horn, W. F. (1999). "Father facts (3rd ed.)." Available from the Internet: *www.fafny.org*.
9. National Responsible Fatherhood Clearinghouse, "What's the 'Buzz' About Parenting." Available from the Internet: *www.fatherhood.gov*.
10. The Future of Children, "Mothers' Economic Conditions and Sources of Support in Fragile Families" as quoted in Regina M. Leidy, "Growing Inequality for Single Parents," July 20, 2012. Available on the Internet: *blogs.princeton.edu*.
11. "What's the 'Buzz' About Parenting"
12. Sarah Allen, Ph.D., and Kerry Daly, Ph.D., "The Effects of Father Involvement: An Updated Research Summary of the Evidence Inventory"
13. Ibid., "The Effects of Father Involvement: An Updated Research Summary of the Evidence Inventory"
14. US D.H.H.S., Bureau of the Census, "The 2012 Statistical Abstract." Available from the Internet: *www.census.gov*.
15. Ibid., "The 2012 Statistical Abstract."
16. Fatherhood Factor, "National Principals Association Report on the State of High Schools" as quoted in "U.S. Fatherless Statistics." Available from the Internet: *fatherhoodfactor.com*.
17. U.S. Department of Health & Human Services Administration for Children and Families Administration on Children, Youth and Families Children's Bureau, "Child Maltreatment 2010." Available from the Internet: *www.acf.hhs.gov*.
18. Gary Smalley and John Trent, Ph.D., *The Blessing* (New York: Pocket Books, 1986), 9.

SESSION 2

1. "Study: 100 Percent Of Americans Lead Secret Lives" October 27, 2004, *The Onion*. Available from the Internet: *www.theonion.com*.
2. "Pitino says he let down his family," ESPN, August 13, 2009. Available on the Internet: *http://sports.espn.go.com*.

SESSION 3

1. *www.goodreads.com*
2. Wayne W. Dyer, *Your Erroneous Zones: Escape negative thinking and take control of your life* (New York: Avon Books, 1995), 259-260.
3. Father's Rights Dallas Attorney, "I Need a Father: A father's role in child custody," October 19, 2010. Available from the Internet: *www.fathersrightsdallas.com*.

SESSION 4

1. Adapted from RJ Young, "The Story of Marcus Dupree," November 9, 2010. Available from the Internet: *www.oudaily.com*.
2. Kent Ninomiya, "What Does It Take to Be an NFL Player?" March 28, 2011. Available from the Internet: *www.livestrong.com*.
3. *www.goodreads.com*
4. C. S. Lewis, *Mere Christianity* (New York: HarperCollins, 2001), 123-124.
5. George Müller, *A Narrative of Some of the Lord's Dealings with George Müller,* as quoted in "The Less We Read." Available from the Internet: *www.bible.org*.

SESSION 5

1. Gregg Matte, *Birds and Bees: a conversation about God, sex, and sexuality* (Nashville: LifeWay Press, 2012), 22, 39.
2. Oscar Wilde, *The Importance of Being Earnest and Other Plays: Lady Windermere's Fan; Salome; A Woman of No Importance; An Ideal Husband; The Importance of Being Earnest* (Oxford UP, 2008), 11.
3. John James Lias, ed., *The book of Judges: with map, notes and introduction* (Cambridge UP, 1902), 168.
5. Mark Regnerus and Jeremy Uecker, *Premarital Sex in America: How Young Americans Meet, Mate, and Think about Marrying* (New York: Oxford University Press, 2011), 168.
5. Gary Langer, "POLL: American Sex Survey," October 21, 2004. Available from the Internet: *www.abcnews.com*.
6. Dietrich Bonhoeffer, *"Creation and Fall" "Temptation": Two Biblical Studies* (New York: Simon & Schuster, 1955), 132.

SESSION 6

1. Sue Augustine, *When Your Past Is Hurting Your Present: Getting Beyond Fears That Hold You Back* (Eugene, OR: Harvest House, 2005), 28.

Threads

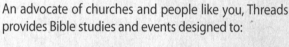

An advocate of churches and people like you, Threads provides Bible studies and events designed to:

cultivate community We need people we can call when the tire's flat or when we get the promotion. And it's those people—the day-in-day-out people—who we want to walk through life with and learn about God from.

provide depth Kiddie pools are for kids. We're looking to dive in, head first, to all the hard-to-talk-about topics, tough questions, and thought-provoking Scriptures. We think this is a good thing, because we're in process. We're becoming. And who we're becoming isn't shallow.

lift up responsibility We are committed to being responsible—doing the right things like recycling and volunteering. And we're also trying to grow in our understanding of what it means to share the gospel, serve the poor, love our neighbors, tithe, and make wise choices about our time, money, and relationships.

encourage connection We're looking for connection with our church, our community, with somebody who's willing to walk along side us and give us a little advice here and there. We'd like opportunities to pour our lives out for others because we're willing to do that walk-along-side thing for someone else, too. We have a lot to learn from people older and younger than us. From the body of Christ.

We're glad you picked up this study. Please come by and visit us at *threadsmedia.com*.

CREATION UNRAVELED
THE GOSPEL ACCORDING TO GENESIS
BY MATT CARTER AND HALIM SUH

The words we read in Genesis are the same words that provided hope for hungry Israelites in the wilderness, breathed courage into the heart of David, and fed the soul of Jesus Himself during His time on earth. God's promises are as relevant today as they were "in the beginning."

Matt Carter serves as lead pastor of The Austin Stone Community Church in Austin, Texas. He and his wife, Jennifer, have three children.

Halim Suh and his wife, Angela, also have three kids. Halim is an elder and pastor of equipping at The Austin Stone Community Church.

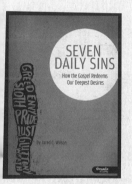

SEVEN DAILY SINS
HOW THE GOSPEL REDEEMS OUR DEEPEST DESIRES
BY JARED C. WILSON

The so-called "seven deadly sins"—lust, greed, envy, sloth, pride, gluttony, wrath—are not merely things we "do," but as Jesus reveals, conditions of our heart. Even if we don't act on them, we carry these desires around every day. How does the gospel address the needs at the root of these sins and empower us to break patterns of bondage to them? *Seven Daily Sins* reveals from Scripture how Christians can experience freedom by the redemptive power of the gospel of Jesus.

Jared C. Wilson is the author of several books, including Gospel Wakefulness *and* Your Jesus Is Too Safe: Outgrowing a Drive-Thru, Feel-Good Savior. *He's the pastor of Middletown Church in Middletown Springs, Vermont. Visit him online at jaredcwilson.com.*

MENTOR
HOW ALONG-THE-WAY DISCIPLESHIP WILL CHANGE YOUR LIFE
BY CHUCK LAWLESS

Drawing from biblical examples like Jesus and His disciples and Paul and Timothy, author Chuck Lawless explores the life-transforming process of a mentoring relationship. This study is both a practical and spiritual guide to biblical mentoring, providing easy-to-model life application for how to have and be a mentor.

Chuck Lawless is professor of Evangelism and Missions and the dean of the Graduate School at Southeastern Baptist Theological Seminary. He's the author of several books, including Spiritual Warfare: Biblical Truth for Victory, Disciple Warriors, *and* Putting on the Armor. *Dr. Lawless is also president of the Lawless Group, a church consulting firm (thelawlessgroup.com).*

FOR FULL DETAILS ON ALL OF THREADS' STUDIES, VISIT *THREADSMEDIA.COM.*

GROUP CONTACT INFORMATION

Name _____ Number _____
E-mail _____

Name _____ Number _____
E-mail _____

Name _____ Number _____
E-mail _____

Name _____ Number _____
E-mail _____

Name _____ Number _____
E-mail _____

Name _____ Number _____
E-mail _____

Name _____ Number _____
E-mail _____

Name _____ Number _____
E-mail _____

Name _____ Number _____
E-mail _____

Name _____ Number _____
E-mail _____

Name _____ Number _____
E-mail _____

GROUP CONTACT INFORMATION

Name _____ Number _____
E-mail _____

Name _____ Number _____
E-mail _____

Name _____ Number _____
E-mail _____

Name _____ Number _____
E-mail _____

Name _____ Number _____
E-mail _____

Name _____ Number _____
E-mail _____

Name _____ Number _____
E-mail _____

Name _____ Number _____
E-mail _____

Name _____ Number _____
E-mail _____

Name _____ Number _____
E-mail _____

Name _____ Number _____
E-mail _____